Stories of the Aspen Practical Joke Years

DON'T GET MAD...
Get Even

JACK BRENDLINGER

outskirtspress
DENVER, COLORADO

Cover Photo © 2014 thinkstockphotos.com. All rights reserved - used with permission.

Interior Images: Jack Brendlinger

Outskirts Press, Inc.
http://www.outskirtspress.com

ISBN: 978-1-4787-3343-0

Outskirts Press and the "OP" logo are trademarks belonging to Outskirts Press, Inc.

PRINTED IN THE UNITED STATES OF AMERICA

Don't Get Mad...GET EVEN
Aspen's Practical Joke Years

Prologue

Aspen, now a mega resort, known in all corners of the world, has had four very distinct periods of existence: a warm delightful summer hunting grounds for the Ute Indians; a Silver-mining boomtown from 1879 to 1893; the Quiet Years after the mining and before 1947 when skiing really got started. It was during this skiing boom that another era got started: the wild, crazy days of Practical Jokes.

Somewhere around the late 1950's the ski pioneering Aspenites realized that their threadbare existence, eeking out a living in a small, almost ghost town, was going to thrive. Enough of the work and worry, it was time to have some fun, especially in the two off-seasons of spring and Indian summer.

With a bit more time on their hands they created fun, sometimes at someone else's expense. Crazy joke stories abounded around the Jerome and Red Onion bars or in front of the Post Office, first in the corner of the Elks Building and later on Spring Street. There was no mail delivery; everyone had their own treasured PO box and the entire town went there around 11 in the morning to get their mail. The Post Master guaranteed, rain or shine, that all the day's mail would be in the boxes by 10:30 a.m. Imagine 900 people showing up for their mail at the same time every day. If you didn't know everybody in town, you did after a couple of weeks of just showing up for your mail. It was an every-day-but-Sunday block party. It was also a major part of the Aspen culture and a perfect venue to catch up, tell jokes and stories. The following chapters are a chronicle of some of the wilder practical-joke stories.

I've told these stories many times in the last forty years, and as a confessed embellisher I'm sure I didn't let facts get in the way of a good story. If some of you victims don't quite remember it "just like that," that's tough! It is the best I can do with this dusty ole' brain.

Before we get to the meat of the stories it would be best that I take a few chapters and introduce you to some of the cast of motley characters of the Get Even Years.

CHAPTER 1

The Bio of Nasty, Conniving Jack Brendlinger

There are several characters in these stories and I guess the best way to introduce them is to write something about each person.

First, there is me, Jack Brendlinger, now celebrating my 42nd anniversary of being age 39. I guess I'm sort of a typical 81-year-old. Can't see shit, hear shit or remember shit. Marsha, my too adorable, too rational wife of 53 years, summed it up when she yelled, "What, you're writing a book about memories? Ha! You can't even remember why you opened the refrigerator door. You stand there so long your runny nose freezes solid. Before you write any damn book, how about cleaning the garage, your closet, your bathroom countertop, and your hunting van —they're all disgusting!"

She's right, you know (or so she tells me every day). But I say what I always say: "OK! OK! I'll get 'er done. Just let me do this one little important thing first!" (Like take a nap). I'll admit it, I'm more than tired in these retired years but I just keep thinking I don't have too many years left so just have fun and don't waste time cleaning anything! It takes me 15 hours to clean my desk and only 10 minutes to mess it up, so what's the use?

The official male life expectancy is 77 years and I'm already past that and using borrowed time from some stiff who didn't make it that far. Why not use that time to write a book, paint a picture or, better yet, take that nap?

I guess pulling off a good practical joke these days is more a pipe-dream then serious action. It's sad when we'd rather just remember the wild and fun times than continue to participate. At least, I'm still remembering something — most of it in the long ago past and nothing five minutes ago.

I grew up in Denver when it was still a small cow town. I loved it and my life in it. There were streetcars, with woven cane seats and clanking bells, weaving down tracks sunk in the cobblestone streets, nickel movies at The Bluebird Theater on East Colfax that always had a newsreel, cartoon and a serial episode of Buck Rogers before the feature. The film was probably a Hope and Crosby road trip to somewhere.

I don't know where all my mischief came from — maybe it's hereditary. I can still remember when I was seven or so the times I was draped over my grandmother's kitchen chair, bare-assed, and taking some well-aimed whacks from an oversized hairbrush. Can't remember the cause but I do remember the consequential effect. I was an imp who was always in trouble and I'm sure I deserved every whack I got.

Even in grade school I liked to steal the girls' lunchboxes and replace the food with a pair of smelly sox or underwear. In the seventh grade I was small, maybe four-and-a-half feet tall. When we were lined up, boys on one side and girls on the other, for the mandatory dance in the gymnasium, everyone else was shy and afraid to make the first move — but not me. I was the first one across the floor to ask Diane Cobb, a sweater-clad, very mature, very well endowed five-foot-10-inch beauty, to dance. I could only dance the two-step but I was the perfect height for the best view in the room.

Junior high school was much the same. In the principal's office, I was working off some sort of punishment (much less severe, however, than my grandmother's) and I noticed a stack of the principal's blank stationary in the wastebasket I was dumping. Figuring I could find some use for it, I commandeered a few pages. It didn't take me long to find a use for it. I typed terrible things like "Your son is flunking everything" about my friends and put them in their parents' mailboxes.

I also typed in all caps, "MEET ME IN MY OFFICE IMMEDIATELY!" and left the letters on the desks of a couple of teachers whom I didn't particularly care for. Especially the English teacher that always complained about my dangling participle (see above). Hell, that was before puberty and I was sure she couldn't even see my dangling participle. Double hell, even after puberty I'm not sure she — well I better not go there!

In college the jokes continued. At the University of Colorado the Kappa Sig house was just across the alley from the Delta Gamma sorority house. Even though several of the brothers were dating the sorority sisters, there was still a bit of rivalry between the two clans.

At their front door they had a tiny vestibule, maybe four-foot square, a seemingly useless little cove that I guess was supposed to keep the ice and snow off the stoop or the smoochers at curfew. Yes, it wasn't that long ago when co-eds had a curfew (couldn't trust them, ya know!). Seems strange now but the curfew was 10 pm on Sunday and weeknights and 1am on Friday and Saturday nights.

Every night at curfew time the Delta Gamma vestibule was a gaggle of smoochers, so that tiny space was a tempting target for the Kappa Sig jokesters. After the first major snowstorm, that temptation was too much. At 3am we shoveled and packed snow and ice into that space until it was as hard as concrete against the front door. The next morning the early class-goers were greeted by a solid wall of snow. It was packed so hard that several days later the sisters were still going through the kitchen to use the backdoor.

One of Delta Gamma's houseboys who cleaned the floors and emptied the trash was a Kappa Sig brother. We convinced him to rig up a microphone in the girl's second-floor bathroom and run a wire across the alley to a second-floor room of the Kappa Sig house. We attached the mike to a tape recorder and hoped to hear and record the D.G.s' incriminating chatter.

Unfortunately, the houseboy had taped the mike on the bottom of a stall between a toilet and the scale. The location was unfortunate because of the noise of the flushing toilet and other disgusting sounds. However, because the mike was near the scale proved to provide weighty material. Almost daily the girls would jump on the scale and usually announce with a groan, "Oh crap, I've put on four pounds — I'm up to 138!" After a while we were able to identify each girl's voice.

Since both houses were on the same street, Pennsylvania Avenue, we used the same sidewalk walking to and from our classes. Encounters were inevitable. I just loved walking behind a group of giggly girls with their bobby sox, penny loafers, oversized daddy shirts and swinging their blossoming poodle skirts. Then with an all-knowing grin, I would say, "Hey, Suzanne, walking behind you I've noticed you have put on four or five pounds. You better watch it or you'll get up to 139. And, Julie, don't you laugh, you're pushing 142."

Good thing I was always quick on my feet because those swinging book bags were dangerously heavy.

There were a few love relationships that were abruptly terminated after a brother heard his girlfriend's recorded remarks following a date, so the girls knew something was awry. Then, after a snowstorm, they noticed an unusual frost-covered wire between the houses and discovered the mike. Knowing the incriminating things they must have said, most of them wouldn't even look at us, let alone speak to us.

They sued us in moot court in the law school for invasion of privacy. We must have had a great lawyer because he got us off — I don't know how because we were blatantly guilty.

There were always jokes going on in the fraternity house. One night while the actives were at a function, we pledges moved all of the furniture out of the house and arranged it in the street just as it was arranged in the house. Another afternoon, during a pledge sneak, we stuffed, and I mean stuffed, the pledge trainer's room with crumpled-up newspapers. When we finished it was absolutely crammed floor to ceiling with wadded newspapers. When he opened his door it was brick solid with newsprint. Newspapers were packed so tightly he had to get a hammer and screwdriver to begin to take them out. It took him hours to find his bed. Several of us took some serious paddling punishment, but it was worth it.

Before I move on to the bios of other Aspen Crazies. I've just got to tell you a great practical joke one of my fraternity brothers played. It was so hilarious it deserves mention here.

Above, I mentioned the houseboy at the sorority house who rigged up the microphone. Today we would call him a nerd but that word didn't exist yet. Neither did the word "geek." We just referred to them as "those idiots with a pocket protector and slide rule." (Don't know what a slide rule is? Ask your grandpa.) We had no handheld calculators. The closest we came to anything of the kind was an adding machine the size of a breadbox (a standard measuring tool in those times). (Don't know what a breadbox is? Ask your grandmother.) This machine had typewriter-type keys with numbers on them. (I'm sure you remember a picture of a typewriter). Numbers were punched in, the add, subtract or multiply key was held down and then the two-foot handle on the side was pulled down, much like the old slot machines in Vegas, and voila, the total popped up on a roll of paper tape. The process was very antiquated but better than an abacus. (Don't know what an abacus is? Ask your great-great-grandpa.)

Back to our nerd: I can't remember his name but I'll call him Percival. Percy had unruly, flaming red hair crammed on top of a bowl of freckles, kind of appropriate for a very smart idiot with a slide rule. His expertise was radio frequencies. He had a Ham radio in both his dorm room and car. His license plate said something weird like WQ3#D, his handle, no doubt. It seems he could send out a radio signal from his car and when he drove along Boulder's high-rent-district streets, the frequency would open the odd garage door, like one in twenty-four or so.

Now Percy didn't have a criminal hair on his stringy, freckled body, but he could and did like to be mischievous. A couple of other brothers and I were with him one warm spring Sunday afternoon, just driving around opening an occasional garage door.

Percy opened one where a middle-aged guy in undershirt, shorts pulled up too high, tennis shoes and black sox was mowing his lawn with a push mower. When his garage door unexpectedly opened, he stopped mowing and stared at it, scratching his head. He started toward the garage to close it. About half way there our grinning Percy closed the door from our hiding place some 150 feet down the street. Confused, the guy shook his head again and returned to his mowing. When he put his hands on the mower handle we signaled the door to open. Percy stopped it and reversed it when the guy took his hands from the mower. He just stood there looking around for some explanation. He was completely bewildered. Then he put his hand on the mower handle and the door began opening. It closed when he took them off the handle. When he alternated his hands on and off the mower, the door opened and closed like a yoyo with the hiccups. We were sick with laughter.

Convinced there was some ghostly association between the mower and the door, he went in the house to get his wife and son plus he called a couple of neighbors over for a demonstration. Proudly, he was going to show off this eerie phenomenon. He put his hands on the mower handle and, of course, nothing happened. He did it again and again and nothing. Shaking their heads, the onlookers went back inside, sure the man was loosing it in the hot sun. When they were all gone, he was completely dejected and defeated he decided to finish mowing his lawn. He put his hands on the handle and his garage door opened.

Gasping for air and with sore abs, we drove away before the men in white suits showed up.

Our conniving Percy went back the next Sunday to demonstrate the fun for other brothers, but his wife was mowing the lawn. He opened and closed the door twice but she totally ignored it.

With several good practical jokes behind me, I graduated; traveled to Europe with Bob Redford (I wonder what ever happened to him?); moved to California; met a fabulous Mormon girl from Provo; moved to Ogden, Utah, to work in a small ski area, Snow Basin; moved to Denver; proposed and married that Provo girl; had an executive position with Martin-Marietta; started a family and pretty much became an upstanding — well maybe an up-sitting — citizen.

Crazy Aspen changed all that when we moved there in 1964 to build and run a 36-room ski lodge, The Applejack Inn.

CHAPTER 2

The one and only... Ken Sterling

No matter what I write it will not do justice to my crazy and fun-loving friend Ken Stirling.

His wife, Martie, was a fantastic writer of humor with several books and magazine articles to her credit. Famous writer Leon Uris said of her, "Humorists are among the rare in the writing community. Martie Sterling is obviously an outstanding one. You have to go back to The Egg and I to find a funnier misadventure. Her book, Days of Stein and Roses is hilarious."

I tried for years to get her to chronicle all these practical-joke stories. But it was hard to fit into her busy writing schedule. Just before she died, she was working on a book she entitled, Memoirs of an Unfit Mother. She never finished it but even the title tells me I would have loved it. I wished she'd had time to write about these practical jokes — she was a real deal writer. In comparison, I'm just a cub reporter still soaking wet behind the dangling participles and subordinate clauses.

Martie called Ken "Iglook" an Eskimo name she hung on him because he loved the outdoors and, being from the chilly Northeast, the colder the better. Martie, a reluctant Pennsylvanian, had been trying to get out of the cold for 20 years before she met Ken and 50 years after. Reluctantly, Ken retired from his Aspen insurance business and moved Martie to sunny Tucson. "To let the bitch fry!" he explained gleefully.

Ken was tall and some would say a handsome man, that is if you liked a too big bulbous nose crammed between narrow-set eyes that squinted so hard you couldn't see the impish gleam therein. He had lips and a mouth, I think, I couldn't really tell. Where his lips should be there was just a blur, flaps moving so fast they reminded me of those soft-tined electric fans that your grandmother told you to never put your finger but you did — once. Ken's lips were constantly spewing humorous, sarcastic and nasty things about someone, anyone within earshot. To a lovable short, Swiss restaurateur, owner of the famous Red Onion, he'd yell, "Kuster, you short little sauerkraut bastard, who's holding you up to the urinal today?"

Like Ken, I was a lodge proprietor and, unlike Ken, a tad on the chubby side maybe more than a tad and chubby on all sides. Ken said I was just shy of a livestock water tank full of horse shit. If he saw me walking into the post office, he'd shout from across the street, "Hey, Hilton, hold your hand up so I can tell if your walking or rolling."

The banter was endless and came at you like 50 caliber rounds from a World War II machine gun. He had a sarcastic nickname for everyone. Nobody — friend, foe, mayor, celebrity, even the revered grand dames of Aspen like Louiva Stapleton, Peggy Roland and, yes, even the grandest of all, Pussy Paepcke — was safe from his scathing sarcasm.

No matter how nasty or disparaging his comments were, everyone loved it and loved him. He was just so damned funny. And, frankly, people adore funny people.

Two of Ken's favorite jokes were renowned among Aspenites. It didn't matter where you ran into him (damn, he'd see you before you had a chance to cross the street or duck into the alley), whether in Tom's market, the Post Office or Sardy's hardware, you knew you were going to be the patsy of some new antic.

These two jokes he preferred to play on the ladies of town because the effect was much more amusing. In front of the Post Office, rain or shine, he'd walk up to some unsuspecting female mark, preferably with lots of spectators and say, "Marsha, do you know how a moron pulls up his socks?"

Marsha would reply innocently, "No, Ken, I don't know how a

moron pulls up his socks."

With a grandiose flourish, Ken would unbuckle his belt, lower his pants to his shoe tops, and there for all to see, in heart-adorned boxer shorts, daintily tug up each sock. The women, depending on their perception of their status in town, would either run away screaming or smack him on the arm and say, "Oh, Ken, you're soooo funny," while checking out his "package." In a few days every woman in town had been a target of this ruse, establishing Ken as a salty, rotten goober pea in town full of fine cashews. Just the way he liked it.

While the ladies where still stinging but giggling about the risqué moron's sox caper, Ken had a new one. In the library, Beck and Bishop's grocery, or anywhere public, he'd walk up to a now more wary Marsha and say, "Hey Marsha have you ever seen a one-eared elephant?" Marsha would tentatively respond, "No, Ken, I never have seen a one-eared elephant."

On that cue, Ken would pull out the liner of one pocket and then reach for his pants zipper. Realizing what he was doing, most ladies would again run off screaming. Occasionally, someone would call his bluff and demand, "OK, Kenny boy, let's see it!"

He would sheepishly begin to shove his pocket back in his pants and start to sidle away. The lady would call, "Ah-ha, so I'm not going to get to see the one-eared elephant after all?" Before he was out of earshot, she'd continue, "Well, it's OK Ken, the word around town is that it's not big enough to see anyway."

Ken was funny, not just now and then but all the time. His wife, Martie, wrote in her book: "Ken had more one liners than Hope, Burns and Carson all rolled into one."

If you bantered with him, and you always did, you knew your repertoire of sarcastic retorts was limited so you'd quickly lose the advantage because Ken, just as TV's Uncle Miltie Beryl used to claim, he "had a million of 'em".

Mischief was Ken's middle name, and you could count on him to do the unexpected, like riding his horse to town with the deliberate intention of riding it not TO the Jerome Bar or Red Onion, but INTO them. He claimed his beer-guzzling horse was thirstier than anyone inside or that he didn't want any of the horses asses who were already in the bar to feel lonely.

After a full afternoon in the bar both horse and rider were also full and searching for the shortest route back to his lodge, The Heatherbed. In their condition the shortest route was not necessarily a straight line. One such evening Ken was bumping around town trying to get home, and he rode his steed into a local lodge's swimming pool and broke his leg — not the horse's, fortunately.

In the late 1950s Ken and Martie left a quite comfortable life in the East where Ken had reluctantly assumed the family's tire business after his father-in-law succumbed to a coronary. Selling tires wasn't Ken's bag so the restless couple toyed with the notion of finding a ski-related business, preferably in the Rocky Mountains. Mensa-smart Martie had won a disgustingly nice pot full of cash in her successful run on a television game show, Tic-Tac-Dough, and they began search-ing the West for an investment. They purchased 4 acres and built a quaint ski lodge and dude ranchette, The Heatherbed, at the bottom of the new ski mountain in the Aspen area, the Highlands.

If you're interested in their hilarious misadventures as neophyte, clueless lodge owners, I recommend Martie's book, Days of Stein and Roses. If you like laugh-out-loud humor, I'll guarantee giggling enjoy-ment for an evening or two or three.

They ran the lodge for several years and sold it thinking of greener, quieter pastures. But after years of round-the-clock toil tending to the lodge guests and a string of nags for guest riding, Ken needed to find an energy outlet so he opened the Ken Sterling Insurance Agency. With his town notoriety and his lovable nature, it was an immediate success and soon most of the family and several others were needed to keep up with their booming business.

Ken finally succumbed to Martie's pleading — no nagging — about more sun and less snow, and they built a beautiful home in Tucson, Arizona. Well into their eighties and becoming infirm, their children moved Ken and Martie back to the Aspen area so they could take care of them. Ken left us in 2010 and when his wit and humor went out of her life, Martie followed her "Iglook" just a few months later.

After Ken died Martie asked if I would speak at his memorial celebration. Because a big crowd was expected, the celebration would be outdoors at the bottom of the Highland's ski slopes. And huge it was!

There were going to be many speakers, and I knew many Ken stories would be told. I wanted to say something beyond the usual "I knew him when" memorial fare so stealing the soliloquy telephone gag comedian Bob Newhart made so famous, I carried on a pretend phone conversation with Ken in heaven.

I regaled the audience with more Ken stories, pranks and counter-pranks in getting even during our 40 years of friendship. Then my cell-phone rang. In disbelief, I answered:

'Hello!" – "This better be important! I'm busy here!"
What? -- Well the same to you fella!"
"Who is this?
"KEN? - You're kidding, Right? Some kind of sick joke or what?"
"Ken huh, How can that be. I'm here speaking at your mem — What?"
"You can see me? How? What? Where? Which cloud"
(I'm scanning around the sky)
"Oh my God…er I mean Oh my gosh. There you are sitting on that cloud. You're all dressed up in a holie sheet"
'What? –No, I meant holie with an ie instead of a y. Your dirty toga is full of holes and I noticed your pants are down around your ankles."
"What? – Oh, that's one of your punishments, I see."

"Ken, I must admit you surprise me, I didn't think you'd – well – Frankly -- BE UP THERE!"

"What? –Uh huh -- You're there on probation. Why is that? – Uh huh -- You were next in line during Michael Jackson entrance interview with St Peter –Yes -- Uh huh and you knew Michael wasn't going to get in so you did what? Yes -- uh huh --you gave them both a hot foot."

"Funny! That's the Ken I know. How'd it turn out – Uh huh –You never saw Michael do a moonwalk that fast. And what about St. Peter?"

"Uh huh -- I see –You never want to give an angel a hot foot who is wearing sandals and can use scary miracles to really get even. I can understand that and why you're on probation"

"Wait, Kuster is here – so who is that short angel with the very dirty toga, rusty metal wings and pork pie hat on top of his halo standing next to you? Oh, Hi Freddie – Did you make those wings yourself? Ah – they're a bit heavy aren't they?"

"What's that Ken? After you gave St Peter a hot foot he put you and Freddie in charge of teaching the angels how to play dirty tricks on the devil. Uh huh –and if it works out you'll get your wings and halo. That's great Ken and right down your alley. I have no doubts you're there to stay."

"So Ken, I'm pretty busy here trying to remember something, anything nice to say about you, so I'd better run along.

"What? -- Uh huh, you called just to talk to all these people. Well, go ahead and I'll repeat it. --- Wait, I can't repeat that – There are women and children here!"

"Ok Ok – I know that's the only way you know how to talk -- Ok I'll just bleep out what I don't want to repeat. Go ahead."

"What the bleeping bleep are all you bleeping people doing here in this bleep hole? I hope it is not a bleeping memorial cuz an old crusty bleep like me doesn't deserve bleep. All you dumb bleeping people must have absolutely nothing worthwhile to do. Get a bleeping job for bleeps sake -- Ta Ta you Crumbums!"

"Oh, And Brendlinger, you bleep. Get the hook —Get off the stage --- Plus bleep you and bleep all the horses Santa ever gave you."

"Thanks a lot Ken, I love you too. But remember Ken, when I get up there I don't get mad ---I get even!"

"What One more thing – Uh huh –Hey that's nice –I'll tell her. Bye Ken."

After I left the podium I walked over to Martie, took her hands in mine, gave her a kiss on the cheek and said, "Ken said to give you a kiss for him and to tell you, nothing's changed, he still loves you very much."

CHAPTER 3

About Peter Greene

Peter Greene is a main character in this chronicle of Aspen pranksters. He was a master joke player. I think he loved catching someone off guard because he liked to giggle. He giggled at most everything and anything, but especially when he pulled one over on you. His giggle was unique; it was almost a trademark. I don't think I ever heard him guffaw or laugh out loud, only a giggle. It wasn't just a he, he, he, it was more guttural and rapid-fire — it sounded like a machine gun with laryngitis. Plus, it could go on and on and on. Bent over and grabbing his stomach, tears flowing, Peter still giggled. It was definitely infectious. Before long, you couldn't help it, you were joining him — no longer about the joke but about how funny Peter was just giggling.

Peter was very fit for his 78 years, sculpted thin from his summer passion of a road-bike ride of 20 to 30 miles every day. He was not a very tall guy, but, he was so crammed full of life, he didn't need to be. His career — hell, I don't know. He was probably in his ninth or tenth career; I'd lost count. He was an entrepreneur's entrepreneur: everything from restaurateur to real estate development. It didn't matter what it was, like a hummingbird to crimson flower, he wholeheartedly jumped in. Peter was a master salesman and even if you were the victim of one of his nastier pranks, he'd sell you the idea that it was somehow your fault.

We lost Peter in December 2010 in a ski accident that broke his neck.

Here is some of what I wrote for Peter's obituary:

"Peter Greene, an Aspen icon and modern pioneer, passed away in Denver on December 27 surrounded by his loving family. He had been injured in a ski accident on Aspen Mountain on December 26 and was flown to Denver for additional emergency treatment. Peter was a fun-loving, jovial, bongo-playing prankster who never met a person who didn't become his immediate and lifelong friend.

He was born John Peter Lewis Charles Grunberg in Amsterdam in 1933 and before he was one, his parents immigrated to the United States and Americanized their family name to Greene. He grew up Back East in New York and Connecticut but the lure of the West drew him to Sun Valley in 1953. In 1956, he was a soldier in the U.S. Army's Mountain and Cold Weather Training Command located in Camp Hale, Colorado, just "over the hill" (albeit 14,000-foot-high ones) from Aspen. The Command was the continuation of the famous 10th Mountain Division that was so instrumental in ousting the German army from the Italian Alps in World War II. Like so many of the Camp Hale soldiers before him, he discovered Aspen in 1956 and moved there in '58. At night Peter was the maitre d' at the famous Red Onion, and during the day he was a ski instructor for the Stein Eriksen Ski School at the Aspen Highlands.

In 1961, already an established Aspenite, Peter met and married Mary Ann Cummings, who remained at his side for nearly 50 years. That same year, Peter and Mary Ann bought and operated the renowned Golden Horn Restaurant and Night Club from Steve Knowlton. They sold it in 1963.

That was the year I met Peter. He owned five prime lots on Main Street where he planned to build a ski lodge, and I was looking for a location to build an inn. I paid him $19,000 for the corner commercially zoned location and agreed to accept a set of lodge building plans, which I didn't need, but Peter could "write off" these now-needless blue prints. Armed with this windfall he and another restaurateur, Tommy Fleck of Aspen's "The Abbey" fame, built and operated a restaurant in Scottsdale called the Cork N' Cleaver, an immediately popular and successful steak and salad bar establishment. Over the next 11 years they expanded their concept into a nationwide chain of 70 restaurants.

In 1967 I was looking for a place to build a primary residence as my expanding family had outgrown the two-bedroom, one-bath "Spider House" on Snowbunny Lane. (More on the Spider House later.) We found a neat "Top of Ridge two-plus-acre lot on West Buttermilk Road and, voilà, it was owned by Peter's partner, Tom Fleck. I bought the lot for $9,000 while Peter and Tommy still had their first Cork under construction. As they grew more and more successful, I claimed that without my "financier" money in their fists they were destined for failure and that they owed me a hefty finder's fee from the profits. They ignored me.

When Peter died, he was 78 years old but with a mind and inclinations of a mischievous teenager. When he wasn't planning a prank he loved to ski and almost every winter day you could find him on his beloved Aspen Mountain hellbent schussing Spar, Gent's Ridge, or Upper and Lower Ruthies. I often accused him of not knowing how to turn. Going way too fast was a trademark, but all of us knew, or thought we knew, he had the ability to handle it. But, in the end, he caught an edge (every skier's nemesis) and fell on his face and broke his neck. Ironically, this happened on the flats below Bonnie's restaurant, a very popular on-mountain cafe in Tourtelotte Park ("Meet me at 1 at Bonnie's") that he and Mary Ann ran for many years with Bonnie Rayburn.

Peter will be missed by every friend that ever met him — perhaps a million of them."

His memorial gathering at the top of the mountain was one of the largest Aspen had ever seen.

Peter was one of my best friends and a worthy prankster opponent.

I miss him a lot!

CHAPTER 4

MERRY CHRISTMAS, BRENDLINGER CHILDREN

The story starts way back when our eldest son Kurt was about 8 years old. He had made a national commercial for Campbell Soup's "Is it Soup Yet?" campaign. He was shown skiing down the mountain, stopping in front of the camera and saying, "Hey Mom ... is it soup yet?"

He was paid Screen Actors Guild wages for the shoot but also shared in the residuals. Eventually he made about $7,000, an enormous sum for most kids ... well, maybe not for some Aspen kids. But $7,000 to entrepreneurial Kurt was just a steppingstone. To opportunistic prankster Ken Sterling, Kurt was a walking, talking piggy bank.

Almost weekly Kurt would come home saying he saw Mr. Sterling and he told Kurt he had two terrific, beautiful horses he'd sell Kurt for the ridiculously low sum of only $7,000. I reminded Kurt that Sterling was a no-good conman who had just sold his lodge and riding stables. His grown kids wouldn't let him sell these two ancient oat-guzzlers, as they had been their pets. Many years earlier they had been good steeds but were now useless, toothless, swayback nags.

Every week Kurt came home with a new Sterling offer, $6,000 then $5,000, then $3,549.99, and my answer was emphatically NO! NO! and NO! Kurt kept his money and I had won.

Or so I thought!

But the stage had been set for the perfect practical joke, and I didn't see it coming. I was blindsided by a Sterling blitz. It happened on Christmas morning.

It was a family ritual that we wouldn't let the kids in the living room to see Santa's gifts until all were decked-out in Red Ryder bathrobes and fuzzy rabbit-eared slippers. In reality it gave tired ole dad (who'd been up most of the night erecting a 5,000-piece Little Suzy Homemaker Kitchen, with working oven, and a 3,000-piece partially assembled Super Duper European Bobsled, complete with a steering wheel) a chance to pry open his Glenlivet glued eyelids and find his Keystone hand-cranked 8-millimeter movie camera to record all the kids' screaming joy.

But this Christmas morning had nothing to do with ritual. There they were, Kurt, 8, Eric, 6, and Dina, 2, lined up near the front door, screaming, leaping, yelling and pointing through the window as they saw the greatest Santa gift of all: two very old and tired horses tied to the doorknob with a huge hand-painted sign around their necks that read, MERRY CHRISTMAS TO THE BRENDLINGER CHILDREN, FROM SANTA CLAUS.

Why, you ask, was this dastardly act the perfect practical joke? For the next three years these nags cost me a fortune in both money and time. I had no corral so I hobbled them and, when he wasn't around I let them run free on my neighbor's pasture. Throughout the winter I had to buy bales and bales of hay, and because one of the old nags had no teeth, I had to break the hay into small pieces and shove the stinking grass down his slobbering throat. I won't mention what I had to do with what came out the other end. I could never find a place downwind for it. If I'd had a truck, it would have ended up on Sterling's porch.

Sapphire, the one with no teeth and sagging belly, could smell oats from a mile away and she would occasionally just disappear — hopefully gone forever. But, no, rancher, Sam Stapleton, at the bottom of the hill and two miles away, would call and say, "Your damn nag is in my oats — again!" With no hindering teeth, Sapphire's experienced gums could easily turn a doorknob or lift a latch. Old she was, dumb she wasn't. Plus, I had to pay that damn Sam an exorbitant price for those damn oats every damn time.

A couple of times a week I had to saddle up the plugs and let the kids climb all over them as I led them around the property. Sapphire's belly sagged so close to the ground you couldn't get the cinch strap under her. It didn't matter, the saddle and the kids just moved to the center via gravity. And all this effort was from a guy who is allergic to horses.

I constantly pleaded and tried to bribe my kids to let me sell the horses. They would have none of it crying, "But, Dad, they were a gift from Santa!" I never had a good answer. I was a dead horseman, a manure-shoveling horseman trying to find somewhere, anywhere downwind!

After that first winter, I couldn't take it anymore and boarded those nags at least 100 miles away over in Crawford for the next two winters Sapphire died that third year, and I convinced the kids that the other one was on oxygen and too sick to come back to Aspen's high elevation.

Typical of kids with gifts from Santa, they just shrugged, accepted it, and went on with their spoiled lives.

Damn that Ken Sterling, I had to get even.

CHAPTER 5

Get Even With Ken No.1

Still steaming from the Santa Claus sting, I was continually looking for a way to get even. One great opportunity came, ironically,
the next Christmas season after the "Merry Christmas, Brendlinger
Children" classic. How appropriate, I gloated.

It was about three weeks before Christmas and all of Aspen's "locals" were putting up the lights and getting permits from the Forest
Service to cut their own trees in the national forest.

I was in Carl's Pharmacy, a hardware, liquor, art supply, beauty,
magazine, book, curios, music, souvenir, gift and toy store on Main
Street. I can't remember why I went in there but it was to get something important from one of the above categories, most likely my
medicine, Glenlivet. While there I met an acquaintance, also a close
friend of Ken's. He looked as if he'd just seen a ghost, shaking and pale
as an albino horse. "What's the matter, John?" I inquired. He launched
into a rapid-fire story about his being a respected lawyer and judge in
Oklahoma and how Ken had exposed him to a horrible experience

that could have cost him his license, his judgeship and after they were gone, most likely his wife and family.

Intrigued, and sensing there might be a "Get Even" opportunity, I told him to tell me all about it. John said Ken had invited him to go along for the ride when Ken went into the forest and cut several Christmas trees for himself and several others. John was delighted to be a part of the adventure.

They had ventured up Independence Pass for several miles. I remarked that the Pass is closed in the winter, but he said Ken knew a way around the barricade. After they had cut several beautiful trees and loaded them in Ken's truck and were headed back to town, John innocently asked Ken how much the tree-cutting Forest Service permits cost. He said Ken had just laughed and said he didn't need no stinkin' permits. John screamed and reminded Ken of his vulnerable legal position and that he could not ride through town with those illegal trees. So Ken had let him off at the city limits and went on his way, leaving a visibly shaken John in his wake.

This was it: time to get even. I went back to my Lodge, stuffed a hanky in my mouth and dialed Ken.

"Hello"

"Hello. Is this Mr. Ken Sterling?

"Yes, it certainly is."

"Well, Mr. Sterling, do you own a green GMC stake truck, license plate ZG 1087?" (I'd borrowed the truck enough to know its particulars.)

Ken paused a beat, "Yes, why do you ask?"

"Mr. Sterling, this is Joe Baker with the U.S. Forest Service, and it was reported that your truck was seen on Independence Pass with a load of illegally cut Christmas trees, and we are wondering if we might come by in the next hour and inspect your property. If need be we could get a warrant."

Another beat, and Ken sputtered, "This is ridiculous. I haven't cut any damn trees — and I damn well don't like being accused of anything. So you can come inspect anything you damn well please!" and he slammed down the receiver.

AHA! ! knew I had him. He'd bit the bait like a grumpy snapping turtle.

Rubbing my hands together, I waited an hour --- then I called him back.

"Hello," Ken's voice was loud, strained and somewhat out of breath.

"Hello, Mr. Sterling, this is Joe Baker over at the Forest Service. I'm calling to inform you that the reporting party is not sure it was your truck that was involved, and I'm calling to say we won't be coming by for a inspection."

Several missed beats, and then in fine Ken manner, demonstrating his elite East Coast Country Club rearing, he spurted, "Who the fuck is this? It better not be you, Brendlinger!"

No longer able to control myself, I pulled the hanky from my mouth and started giggling insanely.

Sterling screamed, "Brendlinger, do you know what I've just done? I've thrown three perfectly good Christmas trees over the bank into the river and ... and," now his voice was at top volume, "I have just stuffed my entire tree, decorations and all into my roaring fireplace with my wife beating me round my head and shoulders and calling me a stupid son of a bitch!"

Grinning at the phone and pumping my fist, I murmured, "Gotcha!"

CHAPTER 6
The World's Greatest Jell-O Mold

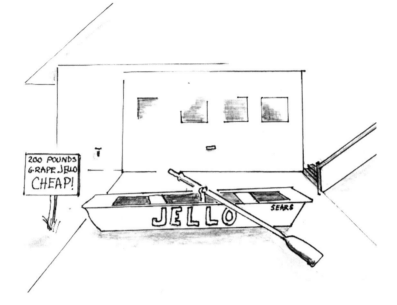

Once a prankster, always a prankster. That was certainly true of Aspen's big three, Peter Greene, Ken Sterling and me. We weren't really satisfied unless someone was miserable at our expense. Our targets were usually one another. Occasionally, however, we would combine our efforts. Victim, beware.

Sometimes when you're in a full-time prankster mode, as Ken and I were, it was best to stop looking warily over your shoulder and instead combine your prankster inclinations to focus on someone else —like Jim Pomeroy.

This tale is longer than other stories here because the setup is necessary, and it's not a bad story in itself.

It began because of Ken's and my love for duck hunting. Neither of us could shoot worth a damn; we always blamed our shotguns' bent barrels. If we both shot and a duck fell, there was a good 10-minute argument about which of us shot it.

The Aspen area was very cold in January and all the pond and still waters were frozen in the greater Roaring Fork and Colorado River valleys. So, if we were going to hunt, we had to travel some 70 miles down to the Colorado River between Silt and Rifle. This section of the big river was very floatable and we would borrow Jim Pomeroy's 15-foot johnboat and float 10 or more miles of river and jump-shoot ducks and geese along the way. We enjoyed this pastime so much that we went two or three times a week. If the hunting wasn't good, it was OK. We had a couple of hours to bullshit, and we were a couple of world-class bullshitters.

We were hunting so often we didn't return Jim's boat after each trip. We just left it in the back of Ken's big ole green stake truck so it would be ready at our whim. We got so we thought we owned it.

We always looked forward to the first hard freeze along the river as it froze up all the ranch ponds and forced all the local ducks onto the river. When that happened the shooting, if not the hitting, would be dynamite. In late January it turned bitterly cold, and we knew the river would be hot. Well, not hot, but cold and hot hunting.

The next morning we were heavily bundled against the subzero temperature and off we went to kill those dangerous attack ducks. Ken always sat in the back and rowed as he didn't trust me with any responsibilities. That was fine with me as rowing looked like work. He also shot from the back, usually right over my head. He always told me not to worry, he'd aim high, and for some odd, queer reason, I believed him. I think he had the last laugh, however, because today my ears ring constantly and my hearing is shot.

We were right: the ultra cold worked and rewarded us with several duck opportunities in the first couple of miles. We were noticing lots of floating ice in the water but the boat was sliding through it nicely. The ducks were numerous and it was so cold they weren't too spooky, and we soon had our limit plus a goose or two.

Then the real excitement started. Around the bend of our usual route the river ran into ice so solid the boat couldn't break through. As any weakling captain would do, I ordered Ken into the river to pull the boat to faster, open water. We still had some 3 miles of river before the Rifle takeout. Once we were in the faster water, we agreed that we had to follow the fast-flowing current or we'd be trapped by the ice.

We were moving fine in the current in a section of the river we had avoided before. Ken poked the bow of the boat into a narrow passage of white rapids bending to the right around an island of trees. Suddenly, we were confronted by a huge cottonwood that had fallen across this torrent. Instinctively, both of us knew of the sieve danger of fallen river debris. If you and your boat hit a partially sunk tree, the water sieves through but you and your boat don't. It is the most common form of river drowning.

When we hit the tree, I was in the bow of the boat, and panicked, I climbed onto the tree limbs in front of me, screaming at Ken to hurry and join me. I glanced behind me and saw the boat being sucked under the tree with Ken struggling to climb forward. With all that heavy clothing and chest waders, he wasn't quick enough and he was sucked under with the boat. In a panic, I threw my gun on shore and laid down on the limb and began frantically searching under the icy water, hoping to grab some part of Ken. Nothing. Oh my god — nothing.

Ken always, and I mean always, wore this old sweat-stained, putrid cowboy hat that had at one time been a nice Stetson but was now a disgusting cap that you'd swear had grown onto and into his head.

Still frantically searching under the water, I noticed the life jackets, ducks, geese and Ken's singular hat had surfaced some 20 yards downstream. Strangely, Ken's hat seemed to be moving slower than the ducks. Ken's hat was still on his head, and because his waders were completely full of freezing water, he was walking on the bottom of the river as it angled up toward more shallow water.

He was out. He was safe — or so we thought,

Remember that the temperature was well below zero and a northern wind was blowing hard. We heard later that the wind chill was 18 below zero. Now we had a new and very serious problem: hypothermia. We were still 3 miles from Rifle with only an old, nearly abandoned dirt road alongside the river.

Ken's chest waders were so full of water he looked like an irritated puffer fish, but we knew he couldn't take them off in the freezing temperature. So I laid him down on the rocks and lifted his legs in the air and dumped the water out.

We still needed to negotiate some of the fast-moving river to get to the shore. I was a volunteer member of Aspen's Mountain Rescue team and had some EMT training and was familiar with hypothermia. But I was still amazed to see how rapidly it was taking Ken down. He started shivering so violently that his knees would buckle and it was difficult for him to walk. We struggled to get him through the river, up the bank and onto the road. He was quickly losing his faculties, and I was dreadfully concerned. We reached the road, and I saw gratefully an old rusty white Ford Sedan parked along the road. It could be Ken's refuge.

I guided Ken across the road and leaned him against the fender. Damn, the door was locked. I went to the side of the road and picked up a softball-sized rock and raised it high to break the little wing window.

"Hey! What the hell do you think you're doing to my car?" a screechy voice yelled at me.

Coming out of the bushes behind me was an old man with some 60 years on his 30-year-old Ford.

I could have kissed him, even on that wrinkly toothless mouth.

As he opened the door, I explained what had happened, and he said he'd seen all the ducks and gear go by in the river and figured something was wrong.

We loaded Ken and drove him to the hospital and he recovered very quickly. Sitting with the old gent as we waited word on Ken, I asked why in the world he was out at the river in such horrible conditions.

He said he was retired (no shit, he's 90!) and that he didn't have money for food and had to fish every day if he was going to eat.

He drove me to a used-clothing store so I could get Ken some dry clothes and when he took me back to Ken's truck, I put the only $200 I had on his dashboard and thanked him from down deep in my heart. A few months later when I was in Rifle, I had his address and thought I would go and see him and maybe lay some more thank-you green on him. There was no answer at his door but a neighbor saw me and said his daughter had moved him to an old folks home in Grand Junction. Good, I thought, at least he's getting three squares without having to fish at 18 below.

Ken, now thawed out, and a few friends went to the accident scene the next day to see if we could salvage the boat. We had a winch and several come-alongs. Only the transom end of the aluminum boat was sticking out of the water below the tree. Much discussion ensued with everyone having a different plan to accomplish the rescue. Tying the winch to back of the boat we tried to "come along" the tree. We ended up yanking the transom from the boat, and Pomeroy's johnboat was lost forever in the depths of the mighty Colorado.

Jim Pomeroy was understandably upset about the loss of his boat, although we had knew he hadn't used it for many years. In fact he was damn near nasty in his demand that we replace it immediately. He was a nagging pest about it, which left him wide-open as a target for a prank.

I ordered a new aluminum johnboat from Sears and after it arrived, Ken and I began to plan our prank to deliver it to Jim.

Jim always bragged that he had an outdoor water spigot that delivered hot water so that he could wash his Suburban any month of the year, including the winter. That hot spigot gave us our idea for a prank.

Since I had a lodge in town, The Applejack Inn, I had food delivered twice a week. When the salesman came by I asked him what the biggest amount of dry Jell-O I could buy. He told me he had a 25-pound box of dry Jell-O that would make 50 gallons of gelatin. Delighted, I ordered 25 pounds of grape Jell-O powder.

In a few days we had a very freezing night, so Ken, David d'Orsey, a friend and neighbor of Jim's, and I met in Pomeroy's driveway at about 2 am with the dry Jell-O and two empty 50-gallon trashcans. We silently hooked up a hose to Jim's prized hot-water spigot and began to stir up 50 gallons of grape Jell-O.

The plan was to pour the mixture into the boat and let it gel in his driveway. But as luck would have it, his unlocked Suburban was sitting invitingly right there in front of us. We opened the back and slid the empty boat across the top of the seats. Then we poured the solution into the boat inside his Suburban; the boat was so heavy it made the tires bulge.

Oh, we were so pleased with ourselves.

But Ken had one more addition to the prank. For many years there was a sex toy that made the rounds at all the Aspen adult birthday parties. It was black, big and had a crank on the bottom of it. You get the idea. It had the appropriate nickname of "Golden Boy." If your birthday gift was in the shape of a shoebox, you didn't open it because you knew what was inside.

Aspen's Golden Boy was better known than the mayor.

After the Jell-O was in the boat, already setting up, and we were ready to leave, Ken produced the coup de grâce, and he carefully imbedded Golden Boy in the Jell-O.

All of us were covered in grape goo. In fact I threw away my now-purple cowboy boots because they were incriminating evidence.

Later that morning Jim's wife, Joan, had to deliver the kids to school. After telling them to go out to the car, she found them pointing and guffawing at the car. Outraged, she dashed back in the house, shook Jim awake, dragged him in his skivvies to the driveway, and said, "Get that damn thing out of my car!" (Oops! We hadn't known it was her car!)

Altogether, they were able to slide the boat out onto the gravel driveway. Joan sped the kids off to school with her arm above the door so the kids couldn't see as she gave Jim the universal salute, exclaiming, "Damn you and damn all your stupid, idiotic friends."

Jim, still perplexed, scratching his head, stood there on that crisp Aspen morning looking at what was undoubtedly The World's Greatest Jell-O Mold. As mad as he was, he couldn't help giggling.

Epilogue: To this day Jim claims we caused his divorce from Joan. He was able to flip the boat over and he turned on his prized hot hose and made the biggest, most beautiful purple Jell-O design. He continued to run hot water on it all day until it was all melted. Unfortunately, he now had the most colorful and only purple gravel driveway in the neighborhood.

The reason for his divorce, he claimed, was ants. Seems that colorful driveway was a giant smorgasbord for millions and millions of ants. Never could get rid of them.

Of course, Ken and I would, biting our cheeks, occasionally ask to borrow his johnboat for hunting. Not surprisingly his response always ended with something like "…and the horse you road in on!"

CHAPTER 7

The Halloween
Motorcycle Caper

County Commissioner Jay Baxter was lying semi-drunk in the ditch, covered with snow-drenched mud and hugging his idling Harley. He was huddled low in the weeds, hoping he wouldn't be discovered by the sheriff's deputy, who had pulled over his completely drunk and giggling riding partner, Peter Greene.

It was a wintery Halloween night in the late 1960s, a time when Aspen was just a few hardy citizens trying to eke out a resort town living and yet have some time for fun — crazy fun.

In Snowbunny, a residential subdivision of local families, the Halloween treat pickings were the best in the Aspen area. Many fathers would accompany their tykes on the "trick or treat" rounds and mothers would stay at home as candy dispensers to the little costumed dispensees.

Aspen, in those days, was a very safe place for kids and adults.

Traditionally, and especially in Snowbunny, the accompanying fathers were offered more libation treats than kids were getting candy. After a few houses all the fathers would be gathered in one home dipping freely in the punchbowl and the kids were on their own, which both the fathers and the kids liked better anyway.

Normally Snowbunny residents were all too familiar with one another and often practical jokes abounded year-round as residents strived to "get even." But Halloween was a prankster's open invitation and the back-story for The Motorcycle Caper.

When the punchbowl was empty, the more-than-tipsy Baxter and Greene thought it would be fun to crank up their motorcycles and go for a midnight ride not on the streets but through the inside of their friends' houses.

Their first house was the Hoffs', Ruthie and Dave's —chosen, I think, because the house was a log Pan Abode and you couldn't hurt it, no matter what you did. Their second choice was a bit more challenging. Marsha and I had abandoned Snowbunny and built a new modern home high on a West Buttermilk Ridge, about two miles from town. Because we were between seasons, funds were low and we hadn't yet built steps to our front door, so there was a temporary plank ramp instead. That ramp was perfect for any wheeled contraption especially two muddy bikes ridden by two muddy drunks. And the drunks knew it.

The Hoffs called in a warning and Marsha and Ann Kevin, our friend and live-in nanny, were pressed to the window hoping that the snow, wind and mud would keep the attackers from our door. I, of course, earlier in the evening, had drained several of the Snowbunny punchbowls and was already in bed dreading the morning "Brendlinger Flu."

Marsha and Ann watched from their lofty perch as two single lights were headed our way, followed shortly by the flashing lights of a Sheriff's car. They were amused, and relieved, to see the deputy chasing, albeit slowly, Peter's bike around and around in the Buttermilk Ski Area's parking lot.

When finally caught, Peter exclaimed, "You can't arrest me! I'm with a county commissioner hiding over there in the ditch." Jay raised his head above the weeds and said with semi bravado, "Uh! Hello Officer Sam, nice night for a ride, huh?" The deputy grinned, shook his head, said a couple of "tsk, tsks," and told both "boys" to stay off the highway and get someone to come and give them a ride home. Relieved and rejuvenated, the riders headed up the muddy road toward our home.

Nobody locked their doors in Aspen, and our front door didn't yet have a lock anyway. So Marsha and Ann had to quickly find a way to prevent the bikers' onslaught.

Our new home also had an entry with a sliding door on the opposite wall from the front door and ramp. They calculated that if they opened the front door and the sliding door at the same time, the riders would just ride right on through to the outside again.

In the meantime, I thought I would fool them by bunching the pillows in my bed to simulate someone sleeping, and I would hide on the deck in my skivvies until they went away. Neither ploy worked.

Constantly giggling, they rode right on in with their muddy bikes and rode all around our circular halls. They didn't know, or care, that I was freezing on the deck with snow piling up on my bare shoulders. They also demanded that we serve some additional alcohol as they were cold and needed something warm.

Shortly one of their wives showed up to give them a ride home. But they still had to get the bikes out of our house. Peter, still giggling, repeatedly tried to start his machine but he just couldn't get it in neutral. Dr. Baxter knew that if you get the weight off the back tire it would start without being in neutral. So, good friend that he was, he lifted the back wheel off the rug with his fingers inside the back fender and said, "Hit it." Peter cranked it and it started immediately —at about 3,000 rpm. The doctor, a good surgeon, by the way, realized his fingers were microns away from being torn off and he dropped the wheel like a hot potato.

Peter, still astride, but not giggling, did the most beautiful, acrobatic wheely, burning rubber on our new indoor-outdoor carpet on his way to smashing into the drywall next to the front door. Beside a burnt carpet and two huge holes in the drywall, all was well.

The next morning I got a call from a very sheepish and weak-voiced Peter.

"Please, please tell me last night was a dream." Did I really burn your carpet and punch holes in the wall with my motorcycle?" I said, exasperated, "Yes, Peter."

There was a long pause and a longer sigh. I thought he was going to say he was sorry but, no, he said, "Oh my god! What in the world am I going to say to my insurance man?"

CHAPTER 8

Get Even with Ken No. 2

It is not difficult to be on the lookout for opportunities. A normal person might not recognize them, but a consummate prankster is always on the alert and ready for action.

In a previous story "The Great Jell-O Mold" I told about our joke on Jim Pomeroy and his 15-foot Johnboat. At Pomeroy's insistence I ordered a replacement boat from Sears and had it delivered to my lodge. When it was delivered it was Aspen's offseason with few, if any, guests in the hotel. So, appropriately, I just put the boat in my indoor swimming pool. What better place to store it.

After selling The Heatherbed Lodge, Sterling opened an insurance office in downtown Aspen. It was in an interior mall in The North Of Nell building. His office was small, 15-foot-square, and was floor-to-ceiling glass on two sides so you could see in from the mall. He loved it. I don't know why because everyone could see him nodding off every afternoon.

But that exposed glass office gave me an idea: Why not deliver that boat to Ken's office while he was out to lunch?

So with the help of Hank, the Denver Post deliveryman, we loaded it onto his truck and took it to the North of Nell. It was noontime and we knew Ken would be in some bar, probably the Onion, having a mostly liquid lunch and chatting up his cronies. We got his office keys from the building manager, who, naturally, wanted to be in on the fun.

We put the 15-foot camouflaged aluminum boat on Ken's desk. It filled up the whole room. Through the glass walls it was beautiful.

But the glass door to the office opened in, and we couldn't close the door. The visual effect was ruined.

We needed to brainstorm a solution. I thought why don't we just push the boat up above the door, close it and let the 15-foot boat fall down behind the door of his 15-foot office? Perfect! Once done, however, the door was jammed shut by the boat and there was absolutely, and I mean absolutely, no way to get into the room.

I couldn't have planned it any better.

Even though we wanted to see Ken's reaction, Hank, the Denver Post guy, and I hightailed it back to the safety of The Applejack inn.

Coming back from lunch, Ken was amazed to see numerous people standing around his office and happily thought they might be customers but couldn't understand why they were pointing and giggling.

Seeing the boat on his desk was not a shock because he knew Brendlinger was the culprit, and he was amused — until he realized there was no way to get into his office, and his phone was ringing!

"Brendlinger, you sonofabitch," he bellowed.

After several frustrating hours of trying to solve the John Boat problem, Ken, still cussing me, shrugged his shoulders, threw up his hands, and reluctantly had a carpenter friend, Jack Van Horn, knock a man-sized hole through the bathroom wall of the adjacent office.

Giggling with a fist pump, I murmured, "Gotcha!"

CHAPTER 9

Get even with Ken: No. 3

I wasn't the only friend who used Ken Sterling as a target. One of Ken's friends came by the lodge one day to show me a device he had bought in a curio shop in Chicago.

About the size of a Zippo lighter, this ingenious electronic device simply went "tweeeeeeeeeeeeeeeeeet." That's all ... just "tweeeeeeeeeeeeeeeeeet," a not too loud but still an annoyingly shrill whistle. Remarkably, it did its little thing randomly. Sometimes a short "tweet" and sometimes a long "tweeeeeeeeeeeeeeeeeet." The intervals between tweets also changed; sometimes it was a couple of minutes, others were several hours.

We loved it and conspired on where to hide it in Sterling's house. I knew that Ken's wife, Martie, had decorated her kitchen with a myriad of copper cooking pots, which all hung precariously above the square counter in the middle of the room. I also knew that, after years and years of cooking at The Heatherbed Lodge, Martie would rather fight the Huns than cook and never ever used any of those decorative pans.

When nobody was at home, we snuck into Ken's and placed that little annoying gadget in the smallest and hardest to reach of the shiny copper pots.

Pleased with the location we waited. Soon there was a tweet, and we were delighted to hear it echo within the pot so that it was impossible to know where the noise was coming from. Perfect!

For the next few days I expected the Sterlings to find the device and, of course, blame me: "Brendlinger, you Sumbitch."

Days, then weeks went by... nothing ... nada.

I snuck into the Sterling home again to see if the device was working. There was the tweet, loud and clear. They had to have heard it — it must be driving them crazy. Still, nothing ... nary a word.

It had been more than a month, and I was concerned that all the Sterling family was deaf.

Then a revelation: At the post office one morning I ran into a close friend, Jack Van Horn. Vannie was a premier ski instructor in winter and a premier contractor in summer. He and I had been high school combatants as wrestlers, he from South High and I from East in Denver. But now, and for many a year, we were good friends. Making conversation, I asked if he had any contracting work lined up. He said he was just finishing a remodel and then he was going to do a project in the Sterling kitchen.

I perked up. "Oh, and what are you doing in the Sterling Kitchen?"

Vannie said, "Martie is very concerned that they have some sort of a screeching animal trapped in their kitchen wall, and she wants me to tear it down and 'get that poor thing out of there.'"

Giggling with a fist pump, I murmured, "Gotcha!"

Biting my lip with glee, I said, "When do you start?" "Monday," Vannie replied.

Great. I had three days to contemplate whether I should let Vannie tear into that wall.

Believe me, after I had weathered three years of the nag horse prank, I wanted that wall to come down. However, my wife's good sense and conscience got to me, so I called Vannie and told him not to tear it down.

I made him promise never to tell the Sterlings who told him that a small tweeting device had been placed among their pot and pans.

He didn't need to tell them who told him — they knew!

"Brendlinger you Sumbitch."

"He, He, He"

CHAPTER 10

Meet Me at Hollywood and Vine

My wife, Marsha, is undoubtedly one of the most caring and wonderful people you could ever hope to know. But I'm prejudiced, so you may want to confirm it with any of the 10 million people in her realm of influence. All of them she considers her family and would invite them to Thanksgiving dinner and give them all a birthday and Christmas present, if my dining table and wallet would let her.

I met this remarkable Marsha during the summer of 1957 in Los Angeles. She was a college sophomore from Provo, Utah, who was working for the summer as a PBX Operator for ABC TV. While we were dating she and I were instrumental in a complicated practical Joke. Our entire apartment complex played a nasty joke on our equally nasty landlady. It endeared Marsha to me because I realized she and I shared the same practical-joker trait we would later use often in places like Aspen.

Let me flash back to 1957 so as to set the stage for a good practical joke. Redford (yeah, that one) and I had just returned from Europe. He had been going to art school in both Paris and Florence and I, just graduated from the University of Colorado, had tagged along, trying to stay out of trouble and to find a place to ski for the winter. We were there about seven months, surprisingly long when I consider how little money we had.

We couldn't even use a popular travel book called Europe on $5 a Day. That was about twice as much as our budget.

While there, living the bohemian life, we were trying to figure out what in the hell we were going to do with our lives when we returned to the real world. We decided that we would move to L.A.

and attempt to get "behind the scenes" of the entertainment movie and television business. Bob is a very good artist and was interested in production design and art direction, using his drawing skills with production storyboards. I had directed some in college productions and would have been very happy in any level of production.

We would need a very cheap place to live and we had asked Bob's stepmother, who lived in Los Angeles, to look around. She found and rented a very small, very cheap, lower-level studio apartment in the Ivar Apartments on Ivar Street, just one block up from the infamous Hollywood and Vine.

The Ivar landlady was aghast at our bohemian looks when Bob and I showed up to move into the apartment. Rose was her name, a short, dumpy, worrisome, meddlesome, middle-aged Jewish clucking hen, always wringing her hands and stammering disapprovals. Our hair was longish and we had several months of beard stubble, and she was positive we were no-good beatniks, and she couldn't wait to find a reason to evict us.

While we were out of the apartment we were sure she was entering it and looking for incriminating evidence. This was confirmed when we deliberately took the full drawers out of our dresser, turned it over, put the drawers back in and returned the dresser upright. This meant, of course, if anyone opened the drawer everything would spill out and be virtually impossible to get all the contents back in. Sure enough, we came home and there was a drawer with shirts and socks sticking out where snooping Rose had tried hard to get it all back in. When confronted, she would claim in a huff that she didn't know what we were talking about.

There was no doubt that Rose hated us. Why she did amazed us as we were soon in the middle of job interviews and had cut our hair and shaven as smooth as light bulbs. Plus, as we soon learned, we were probably the only sane and normal people in the entire apartment house.

One day Rose banged on our door, obviously disturbed, and screamed that she had just rented unit 205 to four very nice, clean-cut, bobby-socked Mormon girls from Utah and that we two bastards should stay away from them. Boy, what a great not-to-be-ignored invitation, so we set sail for the Utah entourage. I don't know, maybe Rose was playing a practical joke on us because it turned out that just a few years later Bob and I were married to two of them.

The craziness of this apartment complex is worth mentioning if for nothing else, it is a good story and lays the groundwork for the elaborate joke. On the third floor of the Ivar Apartments lived a talented quartet jazz band from Texas who was having a tough time getting gigs. It's a good thing all the residents loved jazz, because the band members had part-time, low-paying day jobs, and the only place and time they had to practice was in their apartment until 2 or 3 every morning. Their innovative and hungry drummer, Tommy, would go from door to door in the apartment complex saying he had two pieces of bread and wondered if he could "borrow" a piece of lettuce. Then he would knock on the next door and say he had bread and lettuce and could he "borrow" a slice of cheese. He continued knocking on all the apartment doors until he had a Dagwood sandwich piled high with all kinds of goodies that he shared with the band. His gathering effort inspired the residents to assemble for a potluck supper in the common patio surrounded by the U -shaped building. We did this at least several times a week. Everyone but Rose was invited. From then on no one went hungry.

Also on the third floor lived a beautiful elderly Scottish couple, who mothered everyone, and a retired Italian couple, who made mounds of spaghetti for the potluck. They were the normal ones, and the only tenants Rose liked.

In 301 there were two hookers who worked Hollywood and Sunset boulevards. Actually, they were very nice and, I guess it goes with the territory, very friendly. At one time they were attractive, but now pushing 40 and a bit rough and road-worn, they were just trying to make it while they still could. They normally used a by-the-hour, "pull-down-and-tear-off-sheets" motel down on the Strip to accommodate their work. Occasionally, however, they would bring their John back to the Ivar. Redford and I were in unit 100 at the entrance to the complex and everyone had to pass by our door and picture window to get to their apartment. We always left our door open so we wouldn't miss anything. When one of the hookers went by with a John she would give us a thumbs-up behind his back. Hilarious!

In Apartment 303 was a weird couple in their early fifties, and the male, Herb, was a garment salesman who had an active roving eye and libido to match. Given his homely, bitchy wife, none of us blamed him. At least once a month his wife would go to Palm Springs to visit one of their two daughters for a couple of days. As soon as the cab pulled away from the curb, bald Herb donned his poorly made, ill-fitting toupee and hightailed it down to Sunset to find himself a dolly for the night. He, too, would give us a thumbs-up as he squired his for-rent chickie up to the third floor. No sooner would Herb settle down with his paramour than his other daughter would show up to check on him. We didn't have a phone to warn him and her appearance caused a mayhem of screaming, yelling and door-slamming with the fuming daughter stomping by our door and still berating her wayward father, who was close on her heels, buttoning his pants, toupee askew, and pleading for mercy.

Unit 307 housed Samantha (Sam) a redhead, dyed a shocking orange, and a nose that started at her hairline and seemed to stop at mid-throat. She was Capitol Records' secretary for Frank Sinatra. When "ole blue eyes" came out with a new record, she commandeered enough copies for each of the Ivar apartments. At our potlucks all 30 apartments would put their stereos and speakers in their open front doors, put on the 78, turn up the audio and, on cue, drop the needle. Wow, the senses bombarded with 30 Sinatras wailing at us during dinner and, with mouths full of spaghetti and Chianti, we'd all sing along with "My Way" or "New York, New York." Rose hated it.

Teddy lived in 309. We thought Teddy had come out of the closet when he was three and had a lot of time to get his gay act together. He wore spiky, pointy-toed, patent leather heels below his very tight, shiny black toreador pants. On the top he wore a too tight, too short, white T-shirt that was emblazed with a too graphic printing that would make Eddie Murphy blush. He loved the girls from Utah and, at least once a week, he sashayed into their unit with a homemade bundt cake he'd daintily decorated with multicolored gumdrops. The girls thought he was cute and certainly harmless. Rose hated him!

The second floor had its own weirdoes. There was Billy, a travel agent for a cruise line. Like Sam, he also had flaming red hair that was ultra curly and piled on top his head like a top hat. He was swishy, lock-kneed, limp wristed and elegant! A cross-dresser with exquisite, expensive duds on both sides of the gender barrier, he liked to be the center of attraction and made grandiose, swooshy and hilarious entrances to our potlucks. He would offer Marsha beautiful embroidered women's outfits to wear on our dates. Next door to Billy was a full-bearded, barrel-chested, fledging baritone opera singer and his skinny effeminate boy toy. Nuf said! Rose hated them all.

Most of the ground-floor residents weren't any different. There were two rather plain, horny, overweight Armenian girls from Chicago, that Redford and I named "Olaf and Otto, the Tag Team." They were on a mission to see how many movie stars they could bed. Hanging around the front gates of the movie studios, they weren't too subtle about their calling, but, as far as we knew, their highest ranking "star" conquests were a couple of walk-on wannabes who were crowd extras in Cecile B. Demille's "The Ten Commandments." Not surprisingly, both of them got pregnant and were so happy with the growing bumps of "star" success that they went back to polka away the nine months in South Chicago. Rose hated them and was happy to see them go.

Redford and I were on this floor. While we'd like to think we were steady pillars of the complex, Marsha reminds me that we were the worst of the lot. She may be right — she usually is. But (perhaps reluctantly) she's held on to me for the last 50 plus years.

There was some saneness on the second floor because it was home to the four shiny-nosed, ultra clean-cut college girls from Utah. There was my Marsha, the mother of my children; Lola, Bob's eventual wife and mother of his children; Connie, who later became a fundraiser for handicapped children and staged a wildly successful celebrity tennis tournament in Palm Springs every year. Bob Hope called her the best fundraiser he'd ever met. The fourth girl was pleasingly plump, quite innocent, very huggable, happy-go-lucky, didn't-have-a-clue Joanie. Several years later Marsha and I saw her brother Charlie in Aspen, and we inquired about Joanie. "Haven't you heard?" he proudly blurted, "Joanie, underneath her now-gone baby fat, is absolutely gorgeous and has been voted Mrs. America for the last three years. She kept the title because she was such a phenomenal representative." "No way!" we exclaimed. From his wallet he produced a stunning picture of her. "Wow and wow!"

Before we officially met the Utah tribe, Bob and I couldn't resist Rose's challenge, and we went on a crusade to crassly impress or shock the Mormon coeds. Infrequent job interviews weren't taking much of our time so we had plenty of opportunities to think up dumb, stupid things to spring on the girls as they traipsed by our door. On their way home from their summer jobs at about 5:30 every afternoon, the Mormon Chatty Cathys, all talking at once, could be heard a quarter of a mile down Ivar. It gave us plenty of time to get prepared.

Rose had obviously forewarned them about the nasty Beatnicks in Unit 100 because as they approached they would abruptly stop the chatter and silently tiptoe past our open door glancing in quickly and tentatively. At first we went along with Rose's perception of us and put Far Eastern sitar music on our stereo and in our darkened room we lit incense sticks in front of an electric fan to blow an acrid, pungent odor and billowing blue smoke out from our lair. The next day, with baby-voiced Edith Piaf crooning French ballads, we donned all black clothing, black berets, erected easels and pretended to paint canvasses with pictures of busty nudes. On the third day, bare-chested, we walked on our hands along a five-foot stucco wall. The next afternoon we staged a swordfight (Redford was an accomplished fencer) around and about the gaping girls, whom we ignored as if they were invisible.

As I look back on it now, I realize how immature it must have seemed, even to those newly-out-in-the-world rookies. However, something must have piqued their interest as innocent Joanie came down to see if she could "break the ice with those weirdoes." That evening I was doing the mundane chore of washing the dinner dishes next to an open window. There was a light tap-tap on the screen sash and a cherubic smiling face said, "Hello. What are you doing?"

Shocked, I stammered, "Ah...er...washing these dumb dishes." There went the mysterious cover.

"I'm Joanie — want some help? I like doing dishes! I do them every night back home and I kind of miss it!"

"Sure, come on in — I hate doing them."

Our cool persona was gone and subsequently Joanie introduced us to the take-them-home-to-mother girls upstairs.

Bob and I didn't know it but Lola and Marsha had come to L.A. because their Utah boyfriends had secured summer jobs there, and they wanted to be near them. I don't know if they were trying to create some jealousy but they agreed to go out with us. Things moved rapidly with Bob and Lola, and nosy Rose was having a serious conniption. Since none of the apartment dwellers cared a hoot for Rose, we devised a prank that we knew would drive her up the three-storied-ivied wall.

We staged a mock wedding for Bob and Lola to be held in the common patio of the Ivar. We sent out formal invitations announcing the nuptials to all the residences except Rose, of course. We got a grey-haired distinguished actor friend to act as preacher. Elegant Billy produced the bride's dress and bridesmaid gowns out of his stash and from the cruise line entertainment wardrobe props. The jazz band played the wedding march. Marsha outfitted with Bill's stunning embroidered kimono, and me in Levis under a borrowed white dinner jacket acted as witnesses. Everyone, except Rose, in the apartment building was there, and the ceremony was beautiful and very realistic. Even the Scottish and Italian ladies cried. Surprisingly, Bob and Lola were more than awestruck by the reality of it. Following the "you may kiss the bride," the potluck crew had prepared an impressive reception with lots of canapés and dirt cheap champagne.

All through the ceremony irate and disgusted Rose was glimpsed mumbling to herself and rambling on the third-floor balcony, pacing back and forth like a worried father waiting for his teenaged daughter to come home from her first date. To complete the sham Teddy and the jazz band painted nasty "Just Wed" sayings and tied tin cans and streamers onto my 1950 Ford. Amid flying rice the "newly weds" climbed in the back of the Ford and Marsha and I chauffeured Bob and Lola to their mock honeymoon. We stayed away for a few days, returned and retired to our previous units as if nothing had happened.

Rose was so mad she evicted all of us, the whole apartment house, except the Utah girls, who were leaving for Utah in a few days, and the Scottish and Italian couples.

But the handwriting was on the wall. A year later when Redford was at The American Academy of Theater Arts in New York City, he married Lola. A few years after that, I happily married my practical joker Marsha.

Rose would not have approved! On the other hand, she might have said, "Serves you right, you beatnik bums!"

CHAPTER 11

Detour

Ken Sterling, probably Aspen's biggest jokester, was always on the lookout for an opportunity to "stick it" to one of his friends. He lived on one of Aspen's main thoroughfares, Cemetery Lane.

One night as he was coming home from a party he noticed a road-side pile of yellow and red highway barricades, orange cones and triangular detour signs. Obviously, the Aspen Street Department was going to do some work on Cemetery Lane in the near future.

A first-rate opportunist, Ken knew that his good friend and butt of many of his jokes, Peter Greene, had a nice home that had a large circular driveway on quiet Snowbunny Lane. Pleased with his lucky strike, he gathered up all the detour paraphernalia in his truck, and at the junction of Cemetery lane and Snowbunny Lane he erected barricades and detour signs directing all traffic, both directions, down Snowbunny. Then near Peter's circular drive he put up another barricade and detour sign directing all traffic through and out Peter's circular driveway.

Throughout the night Peter awoke numerous times to the sounds of annoying traffic he had never heard before, but being a groggy, lazy sleeper and a trusting soul, didn't investigate.

Early the next morning the confused police and highway workmen were at his door wondering why in the world he'd moved all the detour equipment and traffic to his front door. Embarrassed, he stammered that he didn't have a clue.

He did have a clue, however, which of his "friends" to blame!

CHAPTER 12

The Little Cliff's Bakery Buns
Or Like Father, Like Son

Bill and Ruth Little had a bakery and it was right across the street from Aspen's ancient Armory Hall, which had been renovated and was now City Hall. Their bakery was long and narrow, housed in a one-story building that began at the alley across from Maddalone's Conoco and ran three-quarters of the block toward the corner. It was painted a putrid bright blue, probably with some cast-aside paint from the trash bin behind Sardy's Hardware.

Physically, Bill and Ruth were the Jack Sprat couple of the bakery business — only in reverse. She was small, fragile with a soft, childlike voice that complemented her inner beauty. Bill, on the other hand, was huge, big as a walk-in refrigerator and had a booming voice to match. Flour dust covered him from head to toe but couldn't hide his enormous smile, which was like a cave in a great pile of donut dough.

His gigantic hands defied what he could do with flour, sugar, water and a little yeast. Oh, those sweet delicacies and delicious breads! He baked buns and desserts for all the restaurants and delivered hot cinnamon buns to the numerous lodges that served breakfast, seven days a week, fifty-two of them a year.

They had a son named Cliff, hence the bakery name, and they were the kind of family that made Aspen unique and so utterly lovable.

Not to be outdone by other town crazies, Bill had more than a bit of a wild streak in him and wasn't beyond poking a bit of fun at someone — or anyone. When cronies came in for a treat or two there was always a bit of funny, sarcastic banter going back and forth. It was a fun place to go and I never missed a chance for some banter and, of course, a sticky bun or two.

Bill had been having some ongoing problems with City Hall — zoning, licensing, or whatever. So, on his birthday and as a sort of cease-fire, he invited the mayor, the council, city manager and a few key employees to come to the bakery at 11am to celebrate his big day. He'd set up a long banquet table on the sidewalk in front of the bakery, chock full of delicious-looking pies.

When the city entourage was in range, Bill slammed a cream pie into the face of the mayor and started an enormous donnybrook of a pie fight. Anger? Lawsuits? No! Everyone had so much fun venting their frustrations that it became an annual event with the whole town enjoying the ruckus.

My teenage son, Kurt, worked in the bakery one summer. His mother and I made the gross error when he was very young in telling him that if he really wanted something and he would work and save his money to buy it, we would match his savings. Secured offer, right? Oh what a mistake that was. Over the next 15 years this little entrepreneur made us 50-percent owners of bb guns, bicycles, go-carts, motorcycles, scooters, stereo systems, a jeep and 10 percent of a 680-acre ranch over in North Park, Colorado.

Kurt was also a chip off the old block because he loved a prank. While he was working at the bakery, he literally loved Bill Little and would get up at 5 am to work at his side with nary a complaint. Not too many teenagers would do that. For some reason Bill started carping on what Kurt was wearing to work. Since whatever he wore was all covered in flour, Kurt knew it was just Bill's way of badgering him for the fun of the badger.

One morning Kurt, not one to sit in the backseat, wore a T-shirt he had cut the back out of so it was really a dickey, an apron — and nothing else. With Ruth and Bill's faces running with laughing tears, he baked the bread, garnished the cupcakes and iced the donuts bare-assed until opening. Then, furthering amusing Bill and Ruth, Kurt waited on customers all day long. Ruth, so afraid he would turn around to get something from the back shelves, stood directly behind him retrieving anything a customer would possibly order from that location. Of course, if Kurt knew the customer well, like the mayor, he did a slow, intentional pirouette.

Young Cliff Little was also working that day and now, 35 years later, every time I see him, he begins to giggle as he recalls Kurt's Bakery Bare Buns.

CHAPTER 13

SMOKE THIS - BUT DON'T INHALE

In 1965 I was playing a game of solo horseshoes in my backyard in Snowbunny…Clang…Clung… when this pale, shiny, baldhead popped up above the fence and made a guestionable remark…

"Do you play horseshoes?"

"Duh! No, I'm using these heavy medal things off a Glydesdale to pound 2 foot long steel stakes in the ground. To make it more challenging I'm trying to pound them in from 40 feet away!"

"Mind if I come over and toss a few with you? "

That was my introduction to George Nelson, next door neighbor, native Coloradan, farmer, civil engineer, surveyor, entrepreneur, gardener, developer, cattleman, certified ski instructor, mountain climber, tennis player, golfer, practical joker, dern good friend……. AND…… dammit!……. a near professional horseshoe pitcher.

I thought I was a pretty good shoe chukker and prided myself with about 20 to 25% ringers, enough to win the Elk's Club horseshoe contest at their family picnic a couple of times. George jumped over the fence that first day and with that tight-lipped determined grin he gave me a lesson in horseshoes I wouldn't soon forget. He averaged about 60 to 65% ringers. Naturally, our games to 21 were short, very short but I didn't like losing, no humiliated, and begged for another game… "Please"! That afternoon, and several other evenings we had time for maybe 10 game sessions. I never won, in fact, I was seldom in the game. It is a good thing we didn't bet or he'd owned my Toyota Land Cruiser, our Applejack lodge plus, I'd had to throw in Marsha and the kids.

Over the next several years I would continually challenge him to see if I'd gotten any better or he'd gotten worse. In either case it didn't happen. Then, many moons later, a miracle happened... and I watched, dumbfounded, as George lost to me (I think he had the Asian flu or maybe a fractured wrist and four of his fingers in splints). I hooted, hollered and leapt around the yard. Then I stopped, cocked my head back, looked at him down my nose and sternly said,

"That's it George, you obviously aren't up to my caliber of horse-shoes and I will never waste my time playing with you again!" **And, I never did!**

George isn't easy to describe...If you knew Darcy Brown, the ex-president of the Aspen Skiing Company, it was easy because they looked like twins. For the 47 years I've known George he has looked exactly the same, from the time he peeked over my fence to his mid eighties. George is timeless. Wiry, in good shape, thin, bald, with a fringe of short tow-headed hair...ears a bit too big, sparkling blue eyes that hide more than a bit of mischief. With slightly bowed legs he has a sidewinding walk that reminds me of a small John Wayne. Confidence comes easy to George, he thinks he can do everything and anything and...he is right. A fiddle–fit octogenarian he still plans a hike up to the top of some fourteener every summer. Most of his con-temporaries, including me, have given up trying to keep up with him. We just find a seat, shake our heads and wish him well.

In Aspen, George ran a civil engineering division of the McCullough Company and he surveyed most of the county. One day, deep in the woods with his transit in tow, George stumbled upon a stash of potted marijuana plants hidden deep in the timber. Being an old gardening farmer, he knew exactly what the leafy plants were and why they were hidden so deep in the woods. Obviously, some hippy was surrepti-tiously cultivating his cash crop.

Now George is as straight as Margaret Thatcher's hatpin, but an opportunity is an opportunity, and with a twinkle in his eye he knew

JACK BRENDLINGER

just what to do with these illegally potted pot pots. He took them back to Snowbunny and replanted them in Peter and MaryAnn Greene's flower boxes situated on either side of their front door. There they were in all their green glory flourishing for the world to see and admire, including the police chief who lived down the street.

Shocked and embarrassed Peter was quick to remove the incriminating growth. He told all the neighbors he had destroyed the evidence. I'm not sure but I think he told me he had burned them. However, that sly smile and constant vacant twinkle in his eye could have been a brewing practical joke or, perhaps, a burn of yard trash that took at least a couple of smoldering months in the environs of his study. You never know!

∞ 56 ∞

CHAPTER 14

Was That Our Honeymoon or a Practical Joke?

In 1960, when Marsha and I were married, couples hadn't lived together for years before they took the leap. (Had that been the case, no woman would have had me and I'd still be a bachelor, and probably a dead one at that!) Most of the time couples didn't really know each other that well. Some, like in our case, didn't even live in the same town during their engagement. In those times a honeymoon was supposed to be a joy, a resting time after the hectic preparation of a major wedding ceremony and partying reception. It was a loving time for a couple to get away from the rest of the world in some beautiful vacation spot, a time to get to know each other better and be both physically and mentally intimate. All Marsha can say about our honeymoon was it was in a beautiful vacation spot, Aspen. Other than that she thought the whole experience was a practical joke I was pulling on her.

We were married in Marsha's hometown, Provo, Utah, a neat little Mormon-dominated college town (Brigham Young University), nestled at the foot of gorgeous Mount Timpanogas and the spectacular Wasatch Range, which rises some 7,000 feet directly to the east. In March the snow-covered peaks are overwhelmingly beautiful.

Our ceremony was in a large community church because I am not a Mormon. The audience was huge and overflowed the church as townspeople were curious to see the heathen Marsha had chosen. All through the ceremony the clueless preacher referred to me as "Dave." "Dave, do you take Marsha," etc. For the last 50 years when she gets mad at me (pretty much an hourly occurrence) I say, "Don't blame me, you're married to some sorry-assed bloke named Dave."

Our reception (a big deal in Utah) was out at a large hall in Mapleton, 25 miles from Provo, and it was even bigger than the wedding. Many attendees were not invited but came anyway to see the spectacle. I think my father-in-law, Max, counted more than 600 people in the reception line, most of them carrying a wedding gift, a crocheted, handmade doily or two. I thought those little tatted white circles would look great on our modern Scandinavian furniture. Most Utah receptions are dominated by finger foods and lots of Jell-O-flavored nonalcoholic punch.

Marsha's dad, Max, by all accounts, was a lovable and revered non-Mormon rascal in the community, and he had cleverly arranged a small room in the back of the hall that was serving liquor in the paper punch cups to accommodate himself and my family who were anything but teetotalers.

I was totally exhausted by all the handshaking, cheek kissing, shoulder thumping and "when was I going to convert" questions. I was also weighted down with hundreds of lacy doilies and couldn't wait to escape. Because of my history of practical jokes I knew my getaway car was in jeopardy but I had hidden my '57 Chevy so well that no one could find it and decorate it. My frustrated friends and wedding party were pissed and I was laughing.

In an unmarked, clean car my bride and I were away to Aspen for a three-day skiing honeymoon. After renting a wedding tux and buying a small bottle of polish for the hand-me-down wedding ring, I didn't have any money for a real extravagant honeymoon. At the reception my grandmother, a savior, slipped me a crisp $100 bill for our honeymoon, and we'd have to make it last. Whew!

Having skied in Aspen numerous times while in high school and college, Mr. know-it-all hadn't made any room reservations because I knew there "was always room at the inn." Uncontrollable urges forced a stop at a small motel in Grand Junction to get to know each other better so we drove into Aspen late and, damn, all the lodges were full. It was Spring Break and the whole bloody town was full. March had gotten popular and nobody told me. We were resigned to drive back to Glenwood Springs when Marsha noticed a vacancy sign on the Aspen Court next to the Chevron Station on Main Street.

In 1960 the Aspen Court was already very old. It was a one-story log-built motel with about six units, and even in college I hadn't stayed there because it was known as a dump. But a vacancy was a vacancy and I quickly pulled into the driveway, eagerly jumped out of the car and trotted into the small office. No one was there and I rang the electric doorbell on the counter to alert someone. I waited and waited, impatiently ringing the bell every now and then. I glanced at Marsha and gave her a palms-up shrug but she was frantically pointing to the front of the car. Confused, I walked to the office door and there was a very drunk lady in a flowery bathrobe and scuffs crawling on the gravel to the office. I helped her struggle to an upright but tilting position at the desk and I asked if she had a room available for three nights. She slurred, "Yesh, but it ... hic ... will be ... hic ... nine dollars."

Happy to have found a room, any room, I gladly counted out $27. She looked confused, counted the money and handed back $18 dollars. "It's ... hic ... three a night." I was delighted at my find but at the same time wondered what in the world could only be worth three dollars a night.

Oh Boy! We should have looked at the room before committing. Rustic we could have tolerated but this was more a wooden Neanderthal cave. It had a small kitchen with linoleum counters curling up like a hibernating bear cub. There were dirty dishes in the stained sink. It was colder than anything hanging off a witch. Obviously concerned, we immediately checked the bed and it appeared to be freshly made but was lumpy and the size of an army cot — but, what the heck, we wouldn't need much room anyway.

The bath was tiny and the walls were un-stripped logs. In the small bath Marsha was getting ready for a sexy grand entrance dressed in her beautiful bouffant negligee. But the billowy transparent material reacted to the rough logs' static electricity and it hopelessly sprang out and attached itself to the bark on all sides of her. She yelled for help and I went to the rescue. I bit my cheek as she looked like a sad ballerina in a tutu and full pirouette. Her negligee, stuck to the wall in every direction, had caused her feet to rise off the floor, and she was suspended like a helium balloon. We finally had to undress her before we could work the material away from the wall.

Finally in bed, we realized that the wall between us and the room next door was very thin and the unit was occupied by a couple of young guys out to conquer every single chickie in the valley. Marsha, to this day, says she learned more about sex listening to the action in that room then she ever did at the knee of her mom. We wanted to move out but we'd spent the precious nine dollars and we'd have to grin and bare it — carefully. On the bright side, three days of beautiful skiing would be our salvation.

The first morning we awoke to the rising sun on the east side of the unit. Strange, because there wasn't a window on the east side. The rays were coming in through the un-chinked cracks between the logs. We lay in bed and laughed. But the sun promised a bright, sunny ski day... perfect!

Three-day lift tickets were $12 each and now we had three days and two nights to go and we still had $61 for Sundeck lunches and romantic, candlelight dinners. We rode The Little Nell t-bar up and skied from there down to the Bell Mountain chairlift. But in that 300-yard distance that the little chain broke and I lost my ski ticket. Marsha and I spent the next hour climbing and searching the slope until I found it. Whew! But, Marsha was thinking, what have I gotten myself into? She didn't know the half of it!

I had met Marsha in Los Angeles, far from a ski slope and confident she'd never see me again, she claimed she had skied a lot back home in Utah. I discovered later that most of her skiing was straight down a slight hill in a Provo Canyon campground. Before our wedding and to make a good impression, she had painted her old wood Northland skis a shiny black so they looked like expensive metal Head skis.

Aspen Mountain is not for the faint of heart and I of course wanted to show her the steeper sides of the mountain. I shoved off and skied something really challenging and when I stopped mid-slope, she was right behind me. I thought, "Great, she can handle anything," and I kept it up all day. I didn't know she couldn't turn worth a damn except for a hockey stop. To keep up with me, she was just going straight down, making dollar signs out of my S-turns.

When we got ready in our $3 room to go out to our romantic dinner, she was exhausted and without help she couldn't get into her nice dress, let alone her underwear. I helped her struggle into her clothes and told her we were going to stop by The Red Onion bar to say hi to some of my college racing buddies, who were now on the professional ski patrol. We entered the bar and my friends wildly welcomed me back to Aspen. We ordered a couple of pitchers and immediately got engrossed in old time ski stories. Suddenly I glanced at the end of the bar and there stood Marsha looking very bored and very alone. Embarrassed that I'd forgotten her, I said, "Hey guys, I want you to meet my friend Marsha!" FRIEND? A few beers and I had already forgotten we'd been married for three days. The evening and party progressed at The Onion and Marsha stayed bored and lonely. We didn't get anywhere near a romantic dinner and later that night at The Aspen Court, while I snored away, she took copious notes on the sex education class going on next door.

The next day I was to meet the patrolmen for a run and just before they arrived I said, "Honey, I told these guys you are a hot skier from Utah so ski the best you ever have just to impress them." I don't know why she didn't just run me through with her ski pole. I deserved it!

For 54 years Marsha has told our honeymoon-from-hell story to anyone sitting down or standing.

Epilogue: After three hot days in the March sun we drove to Denver where I worked as a Traveler's insurance salesman. Before reporting to the office, I had a horrible reaction to all the sun and my lips blew up like the Budweiser blimp and, they were covered in nasty multicolored scabs. I was just home from my honeymoon and I couldn't convince anyone that my Ubangi lips were an allergic reaction to an overdose of sunshine. I weathered their chiding because I knew I deserved it.

I still can't convince Marsha that it wasn't all a grandiose practical joke. Come to think of it, after 53 years of marriage, our honeymoon was sweeter than she thinks it was!

CHAPTER 15

Firearms 101

It is said that the ability to laugh at oneself is an admirable trait. I don't know how admirable it is if you are a stumbling, bumbling klutz and almost anything that happens to you is laughable. I seem to be one of those hapless clowns, especially if you put a firearm anywhere near me. Let me tell you three funny stories about myself that aren't necessarily practical jokes, but given the circumstances they are as good as any joke ever played on me.

Bagging a Trophy: Some hunters hunt for meat to feed their family. Others go through life seeking a bragging-right, trophy-sized animal. I've been both. I've hunted for the thrill of it and ate the meat when successful, but I was always on the hunt for something big and impressive.

One such opportunity came in the late 1960s when a small group of ardent hunters were always scanning the mountainsides surrounding Aspen with powerful spotting scopes, looking for that trophy bull elk. Bob Starodoj, another CU fraternity brother, was working as a bartender for The Abbey restaurant and starting his career as a real estate broker with Mason & Morse. He called one evening to say that he'd spotted a big herd of elk bedding down for the night high on the slopes of steep Highlands Bowl. He said there were two huge bulls in the herd, and he was putting together a group to climb the peak in the dark and sneak up on them at dawn the next morning. He'd contacted me, the Chesley bothers, Jim and Bill, to join him at 4 am for the scramble up the mountain. I had a guest at my lodge who was a U.S. Marine on R & R from a tour in Vietnam. He was in the Aspen area hunting alone, and I asked him if he'd like to join our group the next morning. He was delighted to be included.

The plan was for each of the hunters to drive his vehicle to a parking area along Castle Creek and coordinate an assault team to climb in the heavy timber on each side of the bowl. When the sun rose the team closest to the bulls would take the shot. A big trophy in mind, I was determined to be the highest on the peak and the closest to the bull.

Bob and the Chesleys opted for the route to the south of the bowl, and the marine and I would take the north route up through the heavy timber. The marine didn't have a headlamp and I cautioned him to stay close as it was very steep and pitch black. To add to the challenge, three inches of snow had fallen overnight and the footing was ice-rink treacherous. We were no more than 500 yards into the climb and the marine called out that the 9,000 feet of thin air was too much and he had to return to the Jeep. I, while a bit disappointed for him, continued racing upward to get the first shot. I was dressed lightly but had a daypack full of emergency gear if it was needed.

My rifle was a retrofitted .30-06 Springfield with an Enfield scope that I'd bought from a gunsmith in Glenwood, sighted it in and had confidence in its performance. I slung it over my back so I could use both hands scrambling over the slippery timber, tundra and shale. I was now some 2,200 vertical feet up the peak, and the flickering headlamps across the avalanche track told me I was higher than the hunters to the south.

Enthused, I got overconfident and tried to scramble up a steeper section of scree and stepped on a snow-covered rivulet of ice. Both feet were swept from under me and I bounced down on my butt and back through some 30 feet of nasty rocks and stumps, nearly cascading over a 50-foot cliff. Exhausted and scared, I took inventory and all my extremities were OK. I took a couple of deep, relieved breaths and I was back on my upward quest.

Dawn broke and in the dim light I saw the elk herd just 90 yards above me and still bedded down in the scrub oak. Sticking above the bushes was a huge bull-elk rack with at least seven points on each side. Heart thumping, I realized this enormous creature was only about 125 yards above me. Obviously the resting herd had no clue I was there. I carefully un-slung my rifle, eased down until I was prone, chambered a hollow-point shell and settled into a perfect shooting position awaiting for the herd and my trophy to arise for their breakfast forage.

I didn't have long to wait. As if on some prearranged cue, the bull stood and the rest of the animals followed. Broadside to me, the big guy stretched; he was working out the kinks and I put the crosshairs of my scope in the middle of his chest. "You're mine," deep breath and squeeze. Kaboom, slap, and I knew he'd been hit. I looked over the barrel to watch him fall and lo and behold he was charging uphill without so much as a "howdy do!" I threw in another shell and lobbed a desperate shot in his general direction. Oh God, I'd missed and no one else even got a shot off. I was embarrassed, devastated, and I dejectedly tromped back down to the parking area.

The entourage was impatiently waiting for me and I started to stammer an apology. Starodoj stopped my whining and said, "Look at your scope!" I looked; during my fall in the rocks the mountings had been damaged and the scope was sitting at a 15-degree angle to the barrel. No wonder I'd missed. I felt vindicated and thankfully my comrades seem to understand.

I walked to my blue Toyota Land Cruiser, opened the back to stow my pack and damaged rifle. The marine was half asleep in the passenger seat. I'm always safety-minded and I realized there was still a shell in the chamber and a couple in the magazine and I'd better unload it. I didn't know, however, that my fall had further damaged the rifle's mechanisms. To eject the shells I pushed the safety off and the rifle fired without my touching the trigger, blowing a fist-sized hole in the drivers' door, not two feet from the dozing marine.

I was again dumbfounded, shocked and concerned about the marine. I was trying to apologize but he shut me off saying, "Hell, don't worry about it. I've been shot at in Nam that was much closer than two feet."

I would have liked it if that had been the end of my embarrassing story, but no, the incident spread all over the damn town that the great white hunter Brendlinger had bagged the biggest trophy ever: a blue 3,500-pound Toyota Land Cruiser.

Commemorating my prowess and rubbing salt deep in my wounds, some of my friends presented me with a walnut plaque ornamented with a blue plastic Land Cruiser with a gapping hole in the driver's door. I quickly stored that trophy in the furnace room.

Bearly Feasible No. 1: For the past two decades Aspen has been inundated with a rash of troublesome bears roaming around town and feasting on the garbage. Now I imagine Aspen's garbage is better than most other towns' garbage as the food prices are certainly higher than most. There also had been a boom in the local black bear population, and sometimes climate conditions provide enough food in the wild, so black bears come to town for easy pickings. Several years ago the bear population was controlled by two man-related causes: one was an authorized spring bear hunt and the other was rancher's who were protecting their herds or flocks. Bear hunting is now practically extinct and ranching has been replaced by subdivisions, and the bears (and also the coyotes and mountain lions) are thriving.

Back in 1968, when Marsha and I built a terrific modern house high on the West Buttermilk Ridge, seeing a bear anywhere was a rare happening. We were the first home constructed on the ridge; although we were only three miles from Aspen, it was rural. We didn't know how rural until Papa, Momma and Baby bears discovered that Marsha's cooking was much better and more accessible than the meager berries and occasional carrion they found in the woods, and they invited themselves to a regular complimentary feast at the Brendlingers'.

"Oooh, shame on you!" Baby Bear screamed, "One of you furry black bastards has already eaten my share of Marsha's chocolate-chip cookies!"

In those days there was no trash pickup outside of Aspen, and we stored our trash for a couple of weeks and then loaded it into the back of our Suburban and hauled it to the dump. It was a small price to pay for the joy of living in the country. But then our first pesky bear arrived and took a liking to hanging around and enjoying the feast. We had small children and didn't want a dangerous animal situation, so we called in the forest cops — the DOW (Department of Wildlife). They arrived with a bear trap, a big steel barrel contraption on wheels. They instructed us to put a bunch of garbage and marshmallows in the barrel, set the spring-loaded door and wait for the bear to trap itself.

About 3 am that first night I heard the steel door slam shut and I murmured, "Gotcha." The next morning I went out to check the trap and there was my trapped animal, Herbl, our 175-pound Saint Bernard with a sheepishly grinning mouth crammed full of marshmallows. The next night, with Herbl in tow, our bear tipped over my son's motor-cycle and, in frustration, ate the leather seat. The third night, with Herbl still leashed, we snagged the bear in the trap. The DOW officer tagged its ear and transported the bear over Independence Pass to the Collegiate Mountain Range, some 150 miles away, and released it.

But Marsha's cooking was too much to resist, and the bear was back less than a month later. A DOW officer trapped it again, put a second tag in its ear, took the bear west over McClure Pass and re-leased it in the Ragged Mountains. They told us if the bear returned it would be its third strike and have to be destroyed.

Sure enough, the next spring the same bear was back, but my fam-ily was against reporting it because they didn't want to see it killed. So, to keep the bear out of the trash, I built a 4-by-8-foot bear-proof trash bin out of hefty 4-by-4s, each standing on end and sunk into the ground. Solid as a rock. I devised a locking pulley system to raise the heavy lid so Marsha could dump in the trash with only one hand. I was proud of my handiwork, knowing that our bear in finding noth-ing available to eat would leave for a more productive range. Several weeks went by with no sign of the bear. Through my perseverance, ingenuity and several hundred dollars, I'd won.

However, one bright morning, Marsha, in bathrobe, fuzzy slippers and hair rolled in Coors-can-sized curlers, shuffled out to the trash bin with a full brown paper bag. She confidently tugged on the pulley rope and as the heavy lid rose, so did our two-tagged bear rise out of the garbage. Both the bear and Marsha were so startled that they hauled ass in opposite directions. Not surprisingly, we never saw our bear again.

I of course took advantage of the storytelling opportunity and for years talked about that poor bear with two tags in its ears sitting in the woods near Anchorage and telling the other bears about a frightening adventure on Buttermilk Ridge with the scariest sight it had ever seen peering into the garbage.

Bearly Feasible No. 2 While Aspen continued bear-free through the 1970's, 80's, and most of the 90's, West Buttermilk was inundated with the scavengers. The area had become a quasi-subdivision with beautiful homes built all along the ridge. It was a bear's smorgasbord, and word spread among the bruins. Bears are ingenious in their ability to get into homes, and scary encounters were happening daily. Our house had sliding glass doors leading to our numerous decks. The bears discovered they could grab the bottom of a sliding door and with a strong yank pop the door off the track and saunter in for a sit-down dinner.

No longer frightened, Marsha was shooing them out as if they were flittering houseflies. One afternoon she was showering and when she opened the shower door, naked as a jaybird, there was a bear staring back at her. She had no alternative so she calmly put her hand on its nose and backed him out of the bathroom to the deck. I know that bear is also in Anchorage commiserating with the two-tagged bear "I hear you, man, that was so scary."

The DOW had stopped trapping and relocating the bears as it was futile. Instead they were supplying the homeowners with 12-gauge shotgun shells loaded with rubber pellets about the size of a green pea. They supplied 12-gauge shells but I only had a 20-gauge gun, so I borrowed a 12 gauge from my neighbor, Craton Burkholder, loaded it with three shells in the magazine and propped it next to my bed, ready for action!

About 3 in the morning Marsha shook me. "Jack, Jack," she whispered frantically. "The bear is trying to pull the door off and get in our bedroom. Get up and shoot him!"

Groggily, I said, "What? Where? Oh, my gosh, a bear. Gun? Where're the shells? Yeah, OK! Which way did he go?" Which way did he go?"

Marsha, still whispering, "He's headed toward the hot tub deck. Hurry! Hurry or he'll get away!"

Still asleep and in my skivvies, I stumbled down the dark hall toward the hot tub deck fumbling with the unfamiliar shotgun. I saw the bear leap off the deck, and I rushed to another deck hoping to get a shot as it moved down the hill.

Marsha was upright in bed, crimping the covers under her chin, and heard a kaboom. "Aha, he's got him," she thought. But instead of a triumphant yell, she heard Ow! Ouch! Dammit! Ow. Then a stream of four-letter words she had only read in a Henry Miller novel. Then silence!

"Honey? Are you OK?" There was a long pause then a weak, drawn-out "Yeah, I'm alright — I'll be back to bed shortly."

As I was crawling in bed she said, "Well?"

I sheepishly explained, "I missed getting a shot at the bear, and as I was sleepily trying to unload Craton's unfamiliar gun I accidently shot a hole in the family room ceiling. And all those damn rubber pellets were zing, zing — ricocheting all over the damn room."

To this day Marsha says that it was the fastest I ever repaired anything around the house.

Bearly Feasible No. 3 Two lots up from us on the ridge were Diane Wallace and her husband, Jeff Yusem. Jeff was a real estate developer who traveled a lot, and it seemed that every time he was out of town Diane had a bear catastrophe. I told her to call anytime she had an emergency and ole trusty Jack would come to the rescue.

One afternoon she called and said a big bear had pulled over her birdfeeder and was happily chowing down the seed. I scurried up there with my new 12-gauge shotgun, fully loaded with rubber pellets, and anxious to show those pestering bruins who was their daddy! The DOW claimed the cartridges should not be fired at bears less than 30 feet away as it might break the skin and they'd have a wounded bear on their hands. They also said the rubber pellets stung like hell and the bruised bears would find another territory.

I arrived at Diane's house, stepped out on her deck and blasted the rear end of that bear from about 10 yards. A huge cloud of dust erupted from his butt. There was a loud squeal and he leapt toward the dense brush, but I was too quick and blasted him again. If I'd had been wearing suspenders, my thumbs would have been hooked in them with the pride of a satisfied hunter.

I accepted a gratuity brownie from Diane and hurried home to delight my throng about my "Dudley Do Right" success. I knew in my heart that aching bear was long gone, never to darken our doors again. Our house is perhaps 150 yards from Diane's, and it only took me three minutes to get home, throw open the door and yell, "Honey, your great white hunter is ho ... " I never finished my sentence for there sitting on my hot tub cover was the same bear I'd just shot, happy as a suckling piglet eating a bag of my favorite pretzels. We retired the rubber pellets.

CHAPTER 16
My Jeep is Where?

Peter Greene was a local eccentric icon. He knew everybody ... but it was his nature to know everybody. Peter never met a stranger. In just a few minutes with anyone he made sure they would always be friends. But Peter was the kind of friend you didn't dare trust. His mind was just plain full of mischief.

He once, via expert sleuthing, discovered the address in Mexico of the honeymoon suite of a couple. The bride worked for Peter in the Cork and Cleaver Restaurant chain. With his persuasive charm he paid a Mexican farmer to put a dozen live chickens in the suite a day before the bride and groom were to arrive. He always was thoughtful and generous.

The bride told me some years later that it took three days for the couple to catch all the birds — not to mention the cleanup of the signature piles the birds left behind. Fortunately, it was a tile floor and easily hosed down. Personally, I admired Peter's ingenuity, but thought it was a chicken shit thing to do.

I tell this story because I want you to understand that Peter deserved any of the jokes we played on him. He loved practical jokes, even those where he was victim.

Peter had an old jeep. He loved it. One morning he got up and realized the jeep was missing. Thinking it stolen, he called the cops. They arrived but they already knew where the Jeep was. Someone driving by on Cemetery Lane saw it up on Red Butte Mountain, not 300 yards from Peter's driveway.

Now Red Butte is a very steep mountain ridge on the northwest edge of Aspen and it is full of sedan-sized boulders, steep cliffs and so thick with scrub oak you couldn't penetrate it with a Sherman tank. There is no road on Red Butte, but there was Peter's prized Jeep some 300 feet up on the side of a cliff. It was so precarious that it was teetering. No one could understand how it got there. Obviously, some crazy, and probably drunk person(s) had to have driven it up there during the dark of night. It was so scary even the experienced tow truck driver wouldn't go anywhere near it.

Eventually, five or six hefty neighbors climbed the Butte and stood on the Jeep's running board, steadying it so Peter could get in it. Inch by inch and hour by hour and with the neighbors' gymnastics they got it down.

I know the drunk, crazy persons who drove Peter's jeep up on Red Butte. I wont tell you their names but their initials are:

K—E-N S-T-E-R-L-I-N-G and D-A-V-E H-O-F-F.

CHAPTER 17

Don't Plow Me In

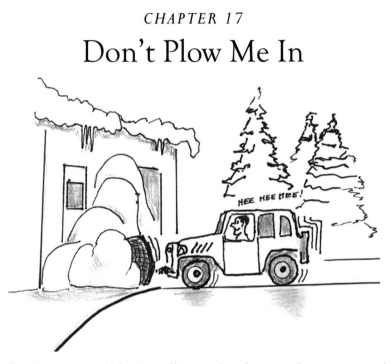

The Greenes and the Brendlingers lived across from one another on Snowbunny Lane. It was only a great combination if you liked to play practical jokes.

One very heavy Aspen winter in the mid-1960s the snow was up to a tall man's earlobes and the dads were shoveling 4 feet of snow off the roofs and making one-story curly-cue slides for the kids. Deep snow is good for sledding, skitching and skiing but lousy for plowing.

Things were safe in Aspen. There was no crime, perhaps because there was only one road in and out of town. Everybody felt safe. The car keys were always in the ignition. The front doors were always unlocked. Everybody charged everything, food, gas, skis, and paid their bills twice a year — at the end of the winter and summer seasons. It was nice. It was comfortable.

But those conditions could always lead to mischief, like this one: One cold night Marsha and I were coming home from a party and since it was bitterly cold, I left my Toyota Land Cruiser running to keep the heater cranking. I wanted it warm while I went to escort the babysitter to the car and drive her home. When we came out, the Toyota was gone. Vanished!

Call the cops? No! There were still lights on at the Greene's and I knew they'd been at the same party. I didn't have to be Jack Webb to know whom the perp was. But, I also knew Peter wouldn't drive it too far as he didn't want to walk very far on a cold night to get home. I walked around the block, found the Toyota, still running, took the sitter home and planned how to get even.

Marsha and I owned the Applejack ski lodge, and I had the Land Cruiser with a plow so I could clear our 36-space parking lot after every snow.

On an early, cold, snowy, dark morning I pulled up in front of the Greene's house in my Toyota Land Cruiser, outfitted with a huge yellow Warner plow with full hydraulics.

Snickering, I began to plow tons of snow in front of Peter's front door and garage doors. I kept pushing snow and pushing snow until I had about 10 feet of snow packed solid in front of both those doors. Gleefully imagining them opening the door later in the morning to a solid wall of frozen snow I went home and, happily, to bed.

Unfortunately, not all practical jokes work out as planned. During the wee hours Peter got a sad call that his dad had died and he was going to have to fly back East — immediately. Fortunately, he had a nice, wishy-washy neighbor across the street with a yellow plow complete with full hydraulics that could quickly undo what had been, potentially, a very good "Get Even."

CHAPTER 18

THE SPIDER HOUSE BLUES

For many years there were no identification signs on any of the Aspen streets except Main. When you asked anyone for their address, they knew, but since no one could identify the streets they'd reply, "We live next door to Louiva" or "We're the white house across the street from the Farneys," and you knew exactly where they lived.

In the late 1950's and into the '60's, Natalie Genoux, an Aspen legend in her time, owned the Little Percent Taxi Company. Since there were no street signs for her drivers to identify, she had a huge aerial, photographed map of Aspen on her office wall. When a call came in for a particular address, she'd just point it out on the map and her drivers knew where to go. It was an early GPS –Genoux Placement System.

One of her aerial landmarks was a peculiar house on the northwest side of town. An enterprising local contractor, who was also a renowned womanizer (I understand Aspen had quite a few in its formulating ski resort years) built a duplex in the Snowbunny subdivision that had long, large beams that stood out from the main structure and, if viewed from the air, they looked like the spindly legs of a spider. As a point of reference for her taxis Natalie deemed it "The Spider House." The nickname stuck until it was sold in 2006 for three million dollars and subsequently razed to make way for a twelve-million-dollar duplex.

Marsha and I with our two boys, Kurt, age 3, and Eric, age 1, came to live in Aspen in July 1964. After selling a very comfortable home in Denver, we discovered there was no acceptable place to rent in booming Aspen. The few available rentals were not only outrageously expensive but also old and shabby! I mean old stick-framed miners cabins that were hastily constructed in the 1880s and, like a tent, set right on the ground with no foundation. As a result, they were tilting drastically to one side or the other, and we could visualize our one-year-old crawling along the lower wall picking up splinters all the way.

These shacks were still heated with a cast-iron, wood-burning stoves smack in the middle of ridiculously small living rooms, placed there for maximum heat throughout the entire 500 square feet. Memories from my great grandmother's ranch house reminded me that pot-bellied stoves glowed crimson hot when fully stoked, and I conjured visions of our two toddlers with bandaged hands and foreheads. We were desperate.

I mentioned our predicament to my Aunt Mabel in Denver, whom I called Auntie Mame because she was way crazier than her Broadway counterpart. She was tall, with long legs reaching all the way to the sidewalk and stunningly beautiful. She was a classy lady who turned heads wherever she roamed, and she did a lot of roaming. Mame changed her hair color daily, depending on what color car she was speeding in or to match the tie of her third, fourth or fifth husband.

Most of her wealth came from an impressive Who's Who lineup of hoodwinked rich husbands. In fact, she went through her second husband's fortune faster than a small leaf in a hurricane, divorced him, and two or three husbands later married him again when he'd come into a new and very substantial inheritance.

Auntie Mame, now intrigued with the need for housing in the Aspen area, checked her ever-present horoscope and found it said she should buy some property — today! So she and her pink hair and gold lamé jumpsuit leapt into her pink corvette with gold wheels, raced to Aspen and overwhelmed a couple of startled realtors. Within a couple of hours she bought the Spider House duplex, kicked out the present tenants, called me and said she had found us a place to live. Whew! I love crazy relatives, especially my Auntie Mame!

We moved into the charming but very small side of the duplex. It obviously had been built as a bachelor pad, maybe 700 or 800 square feet. It had a nice living room with a two-and-a-half-story wall of multicolored, round river rock and beautiful floor-to-ceiling picture windows. There was an eastern view of majestic Aspen Mountain and its daring ski runs and to the south was the breathtaking, eye-popping, snow-covered 14,000-foot Pyramid Peak, framed on both sides by the Highlands and Buttermilk ski mountains. There was a neat sunken kitchen and a practically unusable loft above, accessed only by a steep ladder-like staircase even a fireman would hesitate to negotiate. It had two teeny bedrooms and a teenier bath. We were just a family of four and the accommodations should have been perfectly comfortable.

However, we had hired my brother, Bud, and his pregnant wife, Patsy, to come and work in our new venture, the Applejack Inn, during this first season, and we also engaged a loveable, experienced hotel head housekeeper named Maria Lippert. She was properly Swiss and properly charming with a lilting German accent that contributed to her grandmotherly appeal. Naturally, there was no housing to be had in Aspen and we were forced to have all of them live with us in our cubicle. Maria was about 60 years old and an absolute necessity at the lodge so she needed a good bed and got the master bedroom. Brother and burgeoning sister-in-law were semi-comfortable on the built-in sofas with big, black naugahyde pads. Our toddler sons were in a separate bedroom. They and their mother needed that private space. Marsha and I, the lowest on the totem pole, were up in the loft sleeping in sleeping bags on the hardwood floor under the dining room table. Was someone playing a practical joke on us? Maybe. It certainly felt like it.

Auntie Mame rented the other side of the duplex to the Dick and Barbara Moebius family from San Diego. They were building a new lodge in the village and ski area called Snowmass that was being erected near Aspen.

Marsha had established a little cubbyhole in our loft as an office and she handled all the reservation calls and correspondence for the Applejack. Barbara was doing the same reservations job for their new lodge, and she established a mirror office on the other side of the wall from Marsha's cubbyhole. They quickly discovered that the wall between them was paper-thin and even in normal voice tones they could banter back and forth over their busy typewriters. Barbara was a first-class character, taller than Marsha by a head, very quick-witted with a sarcastic bend, and she, too, was a master of the practical joke. I'm sure she'll crop up later in this chronicle. Hey, but Marsha was every bit her witty equal, so their banter through the wall was constant and hilarious.

"Ha! I can type faster than that."

"No you can't!"

"Yes I can!"

"Nope!"

"Oh yeah, well listen to this!" Rat-a-tat-tat-tat-atat. Rat- a-tat-a-tat-a-tat. Rat-a-tat-tat-tat-atat. Rat- a-tat-a-tat-a-tat. Rat-a-tat-tat-tat-atat. Rat- a-tat-a-tat-a-tat.

"What, you call that speed? You must have sprained fingers on one hand and have molasses on the other —listen to this!" Rat-a-tat-tat-tat-atat. Rat- a-tat-a-tat-a-tat. Rat-a-tat-tat-tat-atat. Rat- a-tat-a-tat-a-tat. Rat-a-tat-tat-tat-atat. Rat- a-tat-a-tat-a-tat.

Then from both sides of the wall came flying rata-a-tats Rat-a-tat-tat-tat-atat. Rat- a-tat-a-tat-a-tat. Rat-a-tat-tat-tat-atat. It sounded like 250 words a minute but neither of them were typing any words just flying their fingers on any and all keys.

Barbara was an animal lover, generally anything with four legs. But her passion was cats and she had several. Neither Marsha nor I care for cats and, in fact, I'm allergic. Marsha didn't like mice either but since we lived in the semi-country at the edge of town, some mice were inevitable. Barbara, however, in practical-joke style, knew Marsha had the mice aversion. Barbara's cats loved her and every day they would go out in the field, catch a live mouse and proudly bring it to their Mama Barbara. Barbara had discovered a secret passageway between the two duplexes (more about that later), and she would bring the cat with live mouse in mouth into Marsha's kitchen and let the beaming cat drop the live offering at Marsha's feet. Barbara loved the ensuing screeching, leaping and cursing as Marsha tried desperately to climb into the fridge.

Spider House Blues II
The Spider house also played a practical joke on me. Earlier in this story I told about the duplex being sold in 2006 for three million dollars and replaced with a twelve-million-dollar duplex. In 1968, while we were still living there but planning to build elsewhere, my Auntie Mame's horoscope dictated "sell," and oh, crap and hindsight be damned, I coulda, shoulda bought that duplex for $30,000. I didn't because it had a small roof leak (ever hear of roof mastic, dummy).

When I turned it down, Mame sold it to Dr. Grossman, who had been our family physician for years in Denver. He purchased a $5 gallon can of Mastic from Sardy's Hardware, repaired the cracks himself, and the roof lasted another 20 years. Instead of me, Dr. Grossman's heirs reaped $3 million dollars.

Oh, those Spider House Blues!

Spider House Blues III

Another Spider House story is worth telling.

In the 1890s Aspen was a booming mining town and a red-light district was an acceptable need in a community dominated by single and needy male rock pounders. Sixty years later as a burgeoning ski resort, Aspen's was full of wild, adventure-seeking souls who weren't very monogamous or even interested in it. Evidently there was a lot switching going on (mind you, not the kind with a sprig from a weeping willow). Amour shenanigans, triangles and quadrangles were happening all over the place. In the morning, bewildered kids would go to school with knapsacks full of toothbrushes and pajamas not sure whose house they'd be going to that afternoon.

In this loose atmosphere, as the story goes, the enterprising builder of the Spider House was having a torrid affair with a married woman, and because her husband was big, burly and nasty, they didn't want to get caught. She must have been very hot because he built the duplex just so he could rent one side to his lover and her husband, and he live in the other. Clever but dangerous.

Besides the big and spider-like beams, the duplex had another unusual feature: a secret passageway was built between the two units through the furnace room. This duplex was on the corner of Snowbunny and Cemetery Lane, and he built it with large floor-to-ceiling picture windows facing down Cemetery Lane, the only access from town. When the contractor's lover's husband was downtown there was a lot of hammering and pounding going on in her side of the duplex. When her husband was coming home sooner than expected, he could be easily spotted on Cemetery Lane with plenty of time for the poundee to repair the carpentry and the pounder to escape via the secret passageway.

I don't know if this qualifies as a practical joke, but just the same there was a victim as a result of someone else's pleasure.

Shameful? Very! But nonetheless ingenious!

CHAPTER 19

The Bare...uh...The Bear Rug Hug

or

Welcoming Peter Home

Seven days a week the Aspen' worker bees sidled up to the grind-stone and just got on with the business at hand. There were only two tourist seasons to make it, and you couldn't rely on luck, you just yanked up your muddy ski boot straps and earned your way. Plus, stow away enough cash for a quick spring trip to Mexico and to eke it through the off-seasons.

In the fall most of us in the lodging business were more fortunate than the bar or retail stores because we had reservation room deposits from the skiers coming the following winter. Aspen was booming in those days and most of the guests would make their winter vacation reservations by September, and send us a deposit. Our lodge, The Applejack Inn had a 75 percent return rate by our ski-season guests. So, when the inevitable off-season came, we knew we would be receiving deposits equaling about 20 percent of the ski-season revenue. Of course prudent lodge owners would put all their deposits in escrow. But I really didn't know any prudent lodge owners. We needed that cash flow to do the repairs, buy new bedspreads, upgrade to color television or paint a few rooms, just to stay ahead on the maintenance curve.

I used to offer free rooms through October and early November to sleep-starved ski bums in exchange for cleaning and painting. These guys were in Aspen for the skiing and just biding their time for the season to start, get a nighttime job waiting tables and ski all day. Aspen was full of them. I housed several of them every fall, but, in retrospect, I'm pretty sure it wasn't the best arrangement for me.

Nearly all of them were college graduates, some MBAs and an occasional PHD. Smart? Oh yes! Carry on a great discussion about Plato and Socrates? You bet! But they didn't know which end of the brush held the paint. Even if they figured it out, they couldn't tell the difference between the window-frame that needed painting from the mirror next to it that didn't. I spent a lot of time, with scraper in hand, sagging shoulders and several tsks-tsks redoing it myself.

Peter Greene and wife, Mary Ann, were no longer a part of the Aspen working class. They didn't need to be. They, as we used to say, "had made it." Tommy Fleck and he had tootled off to Scottsdale with fists full of my money and built a restaurant called the Cork N' Cleaver. It was very successful, and in a few short years they compounded it into a booming national chain. They had definitely made it.

Peter and Mary Ann moved back to Aspen as soon as possible because they still considered it home. It was where they had met and married. Plus, it was the best damn place they had ever been and now, having made it, they could live any damn place they wanted.

They moved into a nice one-story ranch-style home on Snowbunny Lane with their two kids, Katie and Jon Eric, plus a big German shepherd, appropriately named Rommel, who acted like his eponym, even though he didn't have a tank. They all were now a part of the "hood."

Because he was building restaurants all over the place, Peter was traveling a lot, most of the time flying in his slick, pressurized Cessna 320. On one such extended trip, MaryAnn was complaining to the hood that he was gone way too long and she was "REALLY missing him."

Friday night usually meant that it was a time to take a business breather, get some babysitters and go have a relaxing dinner, most likely at The Steak Pit. This particular Friday there were four couples from the Hood: the Oakes, the Hoffs, the Nelsons and the Brendlingers. We all knew Peter was flying home that night and that MaryAnn was really missing him, so we planned to call on them, unannounced, to welcome him home.

When we slowly glided up in front of their house with our engines and car lights off, we saw the house was dark. Damn! Maybe we were too late. Oakes, however, peeked through the pulled drapes recognized the flicker of a big fire in the fireplace. Our timing could be perfect!

But just to crash this romantic scene seemed a bit crass. We had to do something funnier, crazier. The answer was right in front of us on the lawn — kids toys, scooters, trikes, bikes, wagons, and a pogo stick. Each of us found a toy, jumped on it and crashed through the front door screaming, "Welcome home, Peter, welcome home!"

The room was dark except for the fire, and there on a faux polar bear rug in front of the hearth were Peter and MaryAnn, all bear... uh... bare — well, you know what I mean. I have never seen anybody get into bathrobes as fast as they did. What they didn't know was there was a couch between them and us and we really saw very little skin.

Lights on, and there they were, our "marks," sheepishly giggling with bathrobes clutched tight, stammering, "You didn't catch us doing aaaaanything." Yeah, sure! MaryAnn was trying desperately to push her hair fall back up into its former beehive, but now it looked like an abandoned crow's-nest. One of her false eyelashes was in place, but the other was stuck to the middle of her blushing left cheek. Peter, in his haste, had put his bathrobe on inside out. Still trying to be suave and debonair, he was keeping eye contact with us while trying his damndest to stuff his jockey shorts into his pocket that wasn't there.

Since we were welcoming him home, we thought it was as good a reason as any for a party. We broke into his substantial liquor cabinet, poured the single malt and rummaged around in the fridge for snacks.

Hoff, true to his joker form, removed and stole all the toilet seats in the house.

Welcome home, Peter!

CHAPTER 20
You're Invited

The Greenes and the Brendlingers lived across from one another on the infamous Snowbunny Lane. If you liked parties it was a perfect combination. Marsha, MaryAnn and Peter loved to plan and throw parties. I, of course, just liked to go to them, especially if there was going to be endless single malt. Marsha and MaryAnn were, and still are, marvelous cooks and over the years the Greenes and Brendlingers threw some fabulous and memorable parties.

One in particular should be mentioned here because it falls in the practical-joke genre.

The four of us weren't just interested in a party for a party's sake — it had to be different. We sent out formal faux-engraved invitations to about 30 of our friends, inviting them to a black-tie affair. Understand, however, that the Aspen culture was by far more mountain cowboy hillbilly than black tie. In fact, most male Aspenites didn't even own a tie or, if they did, it was usually a string bolo or one so out of style that it was more of a lobster bib than a tie.

But we put out the challenge and, true to Aspen's creative form, they all somehow showed up in black-tie apparel. The women were quasi-elegant in strapless dresses most of which, I imagine, were really bridesmaid gowns they thought they'd never, ever wear again.

I don't know where they got them, but the men were handsomely decked out in rusty but real tuxedos or in time-ridden, red-wine-spotted dinner coats, now more ecru than white. Many of the dresses and tuxes were stretched to their seams' limits. All in all, everyone looked maaaahrvelous, albeit uncomfortable.

The invitation instructed guests to arrive at the Greenes' house at noon. What we didn't tell them was that we had rented 15 tandem bikes for the 30 of them, and after they tentatively and reluctantly mounted up, we gave them a slip of paper with a clue for the first stop of a scavenger hunt around town. All decked out in their artsy-fartsy finest they had to decipher the clues and pedal their fancy asses all over town solving the scavenger puzzle. They looked beautiful, but ridiculous!

The last clue led them to the party site four miles up Castle Creek where the hosts had placed a beautiful 20 foot-long table, grandly set with sparkling white linen tablecloths and napkins, fine china, real silver silverware, champagne flutes, candelabra and monitored by several black-tied, white-gloved waiters standing stiffly at attention with linen cloths draped over their left arm.

All this grandeur was set in the middle of a mountain pasture in knee-deep grass, surrounded by Castle Creek burbling on one side and tall blue spruce on the other, and with an occasional steaming cow patty underfoot!

Naturally, Mary Ann's and Marsha's food was superb and it was served expertly and graciously by the elegant wait staff.

The champagne was poured often and freely, and after dinner we thought things might get a bit out of hand — and they did! Peter and Dave Hoff, the local equipment-rental storeowner, whom we all called "Abby" from Abby Rents fame, began to show some effects from over-imbibing and were commenting on how ugly each other ancient tuxedos were. Dave's was powder blue and a few inches too short at the wrists and ankles making him look like the Gulliver of travel fame. Peter's tux was probably a hand-me-down from his father. Once an elegant black but now badly faded on one side, it was more a dull, blotchy gray. One sarcastic tuxedo comment led to another and a friendly giggling push-and-pull scuffle began. Hoff reached over and tugged on Peter's sleeve and the old tux gave way like an overzealous crowd at a Rolling Stones concert and the sleeve came off. Hoff stood there laughing and triumphantly waving the lonely sleeve round and round. The champagne-sloshed crowd cheered, goading "Yeah — tear it all off"!

In retaliation, Peter grabbed Dave's collar and silken lapel and tore them off. For the next 10 minutes, with the whole crowd roaring and urging them on, they stood there toe to toe, both wildly giggling non-stop and tore each other's suits totally off.

They didn't stop until they were stooped over, hands on knees, exhausted and inglorious, in their white Y-front skivvies, signifying the end of another very successful Greene-Brendlinger Party.

CHAPTER 21

If You Don't Want Me To, I Won't Tell Anyone

We sold the Applejack Inn in 1975. Our guests drove us out of the lodging business. Nearly 75 percent of our guests returned every winter and most of them became good friends, so we'd fly our Cessna 210 all over the country and visit them in the spring and fall.

In 1964 when we opened the lodge we started two weekly traditions. One was a glühwein après-ski party at the lodge on Monday afternoon that was very popular because all the guests could reestablish their relationships with other guests from years before. The other tradition proved to be our eventual downfall, a weekly cocktail party at our home.

The Applejack Inn had 36 rooms and except for Christmas and school breaks when the lodge was filled with families, our occupancy was usually 36 couples. A cocktail party for 72 was not a problem because Marsha is an Aspen version of Martha Stewart and the Barefoot Contessa all rolled into one. Entertaining for her is as easy as mixing a jug of Kool-Aid. However, if you entertain 36 couples two nights a week, they, individually, want to reciprocate and invite you to dinner the other five nights. Logistically, it was impossible. We had four children — enough said! Week after week, year after year of declining dinner invitations, we were making our guests mad instead of happy.

Our dilemma of being too popular with our guests, plus not being able to find good housemaids, plus my own inability to stick with any career longer than 10 years led to a sale.

Aspenites are always looking for a reason to party and if they can't find one, that's a good enough reason to have one. The closing of the Applejack the spring we sold it was a fabulous reason. Our friends threw us a surprise party at the lodge about two weeks after we closed for the offseason. The new owners were to take over the first of June.

The party was a potluck affair around the indoor pool and there were about forty people. Because of the indoor pool and the fact that there were going to be alcohol-pickled partiers, most everyone brought swimsuits as a precaution to the inevitable. Sure enough, the party wasn't even warmed up when the first clothed person was "accidently" thrown in the pool. Much like a NASCAR pit crew, there was a mad dash of the dry guests to a couple of guestrooms for a change to swim attire.

I said most of the guests had thought of swimsuits — everyone but Bette Oakes, who, as usual, was decked out in her New York-style finery, furs and all. She knew she was going to get wet so she thought it would be better in bra and panties than her designer togs. She went upstairs to a guestroom she thought was the one the ladies had been changing in. Wrong! She was in one the men had used. While she was undressing, the sliding door slide open and Chuck Cole came in. Bette ducked down behind the bed and, in the semi-dark room, he didn't see her and he quickly started to strip. At first she didn't know what to do and waited too long until Chuck was down to nothing. Bette decided she should warn him and she squeaked, "If you don't want me to, I won't tell anyone."

To this day Chuck claims that it was a compliment, and Bette, when quizzed, with a sparkle in her eye just silently smiles.

Sometimes a practical joke just happens; no one has planned it. Since the Applejack had been closed for two weeks I hadn't been maintaining the pool with the usual chemicals. Even though it looked clear and clean, it wasn't. Sally Cole, a blond fun-loving aristocrat from Shaker Heights, Ohio, was the first clothed person "knocked" into the pool. She was wearing a beautiful creamy cashmere pantsuit. After a half hour or so in the warm water, the size 6 petite suit would fit a 300-pound pulling guard and had changed color to a putrid khaki that glowed. The chemicals or lack thereof also turned everyone's hair and swimsuits to a shade of fluorescent lime. Blonde Sally vainly tried to wash out her green hair but in its own good time, it just had to grow out.

Goodbye Applejack Inn— it was nice to know you!

CHAPTER 22

Whose Clothes Are These Anyway?

GERONIMO

I'm not known as a person who gets things done overnight. When I was in business, menial chores got done but usually at a slower, reasonable pace. Suggest a tee time, or a fishing date, however, and I'm a whirlwind of attentive activity.

In 1968 Marsha and I built a nice five bedroom modern home up on the ridge of West Buttermilk. In fact, we were pioneers of sort as ours was the first house to be built up there. It was a spectacular and unusual home on a spectacular and unusual site. To our delight, Architectural Digest sent a photographer to chronicle it for an article and it was a hit on the annual House and Garden Tour.

During construction the contractor said we could save a lot of money if we did some of the finishing work ourselves. To Marsha's chagrin I jumped at the chance to paint the insides of the closets, build the steps to the front door and the back deck for a Jacuzzi. It took me only two years to build the steps and four years to build the deck and spa. In fact, during the next 33 years I never did paint the insides of the closets. Besides Marsha, no one else ever noticed. However, she did notice and sometimes three or four times a day she would complain about it. I'm glad I didn't paint them. It would have been a waste of time and paint because after we sold the house in 2002, the buyers tore it down and erected a 19,000-square-foot, 42-million-dollar, French-styled mansion in its place. When we toured the finished chateau, I peeked curiously into the closets and every damn one of them was painted.

For months — no years — after we moved in, I had been telling our friends how neat the spa at our new Buttermilk home was going to be as it would have a 280-degree view of the entire Aspen Valley and the lofty 14,000-foot peaks of the Continental Divide. They said they couldn't wait, but they all knew me well and knew they'd have to.

Finally after I had been crowing for several years, I announced proudly that the deck was finished and the Jacuzzi spa would be full and hot by Saturday night, and our friends could schedule a soak and a libation.

Surprisingly, none of our circle said they'd come up for a tub. Late on Saturday night we found out why. The group had been out to a steak dinner and, as usual, had drunk a keg of wine to wash it down. More than tipsy, they all showed up en masse. If my memory serves me, I think it was the Hopkins, Zanins, Oakes, Stapletons, Reeses and the Andersons. Most of them brought a bathing suit, flippers and snorkels to christen the long-awaited spa. They changed into their suits in a couple of the bedrooms. David Stapleton, all 180 pounds of him, forgot a suit, but rummaging around in one of the bedrooms he found our 9-year-old daughter's two-piece bikini. Somehow he squirreled his way into both the top and bottom, looking sort of like those fat ladies in butt-floss thongs we see on "The Biggest Loser." Sadly, no one thought to get a picture of Dave — it would be worth a ton of bribery money today.

Like pod peas, eleven of them crammed into the Jacuzzi that the brochure said was for eight. Scotch or wine all around, they were having a very good time.

John Oakes, however, had not gotten in and was fully clothed and dapper, sitting very kinglike in a reclining deckchair. Always the protagonist, Deric Hopkins couldn't stand that and started splashing water on him and goading him to jump in, calling him a pussy. John, in his usual quiet manner, moved his chair back but he couldn't get far enough away to keep from getting wet and enduring Deric's tirade. Quietly, he simply arose and went inside. That was that! Or, so we thought!

A few minutes later the sliding door opened with a slam and John, fully dressed, came busting out with a Geronimo war cry and cannonballed into the spa. Everyone laughed and laughed at John, sopping wet, flopping around in all his clothes.

All but Deric.

"Wait a minute, wait a minute," Deric screamed. "Those ... those are my clothes, and those are my Gucci shoes ... and that is my new Omega wristwatch!"

Yeah, John, don't get mad — get even!

CHAPTER 23

Where's the Beef?

In the late 1960's and early 70's, Peter Greene and Tommy Fleck were building Cork N' Cleaver restaurants all over the country and if any of the new ones were within a tank of gas they invited their hard-core Aspen friends to the grand openings.

As I recall this group of chosen Aspenites were the Brendlingers, the Andersons, the Oakes, the Hoffs, the Hopkins, the Sterlings, the Reeses, the Zanins and a few others. Why in the world they invited this nasty group was beyond all of us. They must have known we wouldn't just come nicely to the party. That would be boring and certainly out of character.

Peter was opening a new "Cork" on the west side of Denver near a new shopping center, and he invited all of us to the Grand Opening. I think the restaurant seated about 110 diners and our group from

Aspen made up about one-quarter of the capacity. In our honor, they had arranged a huge table that would accommodate all of us. Since all the cocktails and steaks were to be on the house, the Aspen entourage was the first to arrive and got into the single malt immediately and heavily.

When the waiters came by to take our food orders, we stalled, hemmed and hawed, and said "Come back later" and had another six-dollar 12-year-old Glenlivet on the rocks.

When the party and our table was at its peak, there was a loud, blaring trumpet fanfare at the front door. TA DA... TA DA! Everything stopped.

On cue, all the Aspenites cheered, pulled out and donned McDonald's paper skullcaps, paper McDonald's bibs and watched six McDonald's-attired delivery boys march in with towels over their arm and huge overloaded trays with silver-covered dishes. With great flair they placed a covered dish in front of each of the Aspen guests. The delivery boys pulled off the covers in unison and revealed twenty-four Big Macs to our cheering, hungry crowd. Plus, they grandly presented Happy Meals and fries to a stunned Mary Ann, Peter and Tommy.

Of course, the McDonald's waiters were actually local actors we had hired. We preferred Ronald McDonald as the spiritual leader of this group but we couldn't find an appropriate costume.

The rest of the Cork's guests roared at our prank, but Peter got the last laugh: he refused to serve us any steaks and we were forced to choke down our Happy Meal prank.

In unison we cried, "Where's the Beef?"

CHAPTER 24

Help...My Transmission is Gone (Or Peter's Jeep Joke #2)

Aspen was still pretty small in the mid-to late 1960s, about 900 residents. The boom was on however, and the population was now beginning to teem, but there was still a hardy core of fun characters with a hell-bent fervor for socializing. People were building houses everywhere. Every weekend there was a housewarming party attended by one and all.

We were at a housewarming party for a new home the McBrides, Laurie and John, had built high up on the right side of the tracks: Red Mountain. During the evening Dave Hoff, another jokester of some fame, with his trusty wrench and screwdriver went around and secretly removed all the toilet seats in the new house and hid them down the hill. Also prankster Peter Greene overheard McBride complain that with all the people in the house it was too warm and someone should open the front door. Peter obliged, opened the front door, took it off its hinges and hid it down the hill with the toilet seats. Since it was way below zero outside it didn't stay warm inside for very long.

However, one bad deed deserves another and little did I know how justifying fate can be.

It was a great party, even though the ladies had to pee standing up (served those lazy broads, right?)

Marsha and I had to leave the McBrides' early because of babysitter problems and when we got to our car I realized Peter Greene's unlocked Land Cruiser was there and just asking for a joke. I couldn't remember why but I knew I owed Peter a prank. But then again I always owed Peter a "get even." I had in my jeep one of those big bumper jacks so I quickly jacked up his jeep so the back tires were just barely off the ground and put a couple of big construction blocks under the frame. When Peter popped the clutch nothing would happen.

However, I knew he had four-wheel drive and the jeep was sitting at an odd angle. He might notice and engage the front wheels and just drive off the blocks. Not satisfied, I unlocked the winch built into the front of his jeep and pulled the steel cable back under his car and hooked it to the car bumper parked right behind him and relocked the winch.

A few days later I saw Peter and he started to tell me what a terrible thing Ken Sterling had done to him at the McBrides' party. (Ken wasn't even at the party, but Peter blamed Ken for anything and everything.) Aha, I thought, two birds with one stone — all the better. I listened intently throwing in an occasional tsk, tsk. His elderly mother, "Nanny" Greene, a pistol in her own right, was visiting, and he and MaryAnn had brought her to the McBrides' party. She was a Greene; she liked to party.

With his mom in the back seat Peter didn't notice the blocks and sat there revving the engine and cussing away that his transmission was gone. Another guest saw the blocks under the frame and suggested Peter engage the front-wheel drive and drive off the blocks. He did. Nanny started to giggle. Relieved his transmission was okay, Peter tried to pull out, then tightening the winch cable his Toyota still wouldn't move. He just sat there while all four wheels were laying down rubber but still not moving forward.

Nanny with her pillbox hat askew and white-gloved hands over mouth was stifling a guffaw. Pissed now, Peter put the transmission in low-low, revved the engine to the red line and violently popped the clutch ... and tore the front bumper clean off Dave Hoff's car.

It didn't help much that Nanny Greene, in the back seat, was laughing her little, wrinkly ass off.

Tsk! Tsk!

Both Hoff and Peter hounded Ken to pay for the damage to their cars, and neither one believed his snickering pleas of innocence.

It was several merciful years later that I told Peter it was me and not Ken. I still haven't told Hoff.

CHAPTER 25

How long is your hose anyway!

Seems like there was always something weird or funny going on in the Snowbunny "hood." Peter Greene, a member of the hood, was an imp and always on the lookout for mischief. He never went to a party that he didn't short sheet every bed in every bedroom of the host. Since none of us locked our houses, it wasn't unusual for him to sneak into your house and commit some dastardly deeds: remove and hide all your pots and pans or just the forks and spoons. Ever try to eat soup with a knife?

On one of those typical warm, bright, and sunny Indian summer afternoons, so cherished in Aspen, Marsha, who was eight months pregnant with our daughter Dina, was out in the middle of the gravel street between the Greene's and Brendlinger's houses. Peter was watering his newly seeded front lawn with a garden hose that was at least 100 feet long. Marsha was probably trying to round up her two boys, who, like the rest of the hood kids, had the run of anything and anywhere within 1000 yards of home.

As usual, she and Peter were engrossed in sarcastic verbal barbs traded back and forth. Now picture this: Marsha was big —so big she cast an enormous shadow, so large you'd swear the Goodyear blimp was overhead coming around the corner. When she walked she waddled like a gimpy goose, when she tried to run she was a runaway octopus on steroids.

Peter evidently took exception to something Marsha did or said because he jumped his knee-high fence with his long spurting water hose and started chasing the fleeing, screaming, scrambling octopus Marsha down Snowbunny Lane. Marsha's yelling sounded more like a high-pitched laugh than screeching, and Peter was snorting his patented giggle. Just as he was catching up and about to drench her, he ran out of hose. Stretched to its full length, the hose sprang and slung him onto his back in the middle of the street with the water, geyser-style, shooting straight up, soaking him instead of Marsha.

For many, many years Marsha teased him, "Peter, let's face it, your hose just isn't long enough!"

CHAPTER 26

Hello... Hello... Hello... Hello!

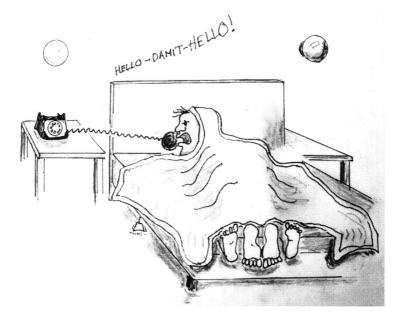

A practical joke that turns out better than anyone could expect is, by far, the best of all.

As proprietor of the Applejack I sometimes got unusual requests from friends and past guests.

A Chicago friend of mine from college who had stayed with me a few nights shortly after we opened called with one very unusual, but potentially hilarious, practical joke request.

He was to be a best man at a friend's wedding and he, surreptitiously, discovered they were coming to Aspen on their skiing honeymoon, and they were going to stay at his friend's Applejack Inn for a week. However the newlyweds had no idea their best man knew anyone in Aspen, let alone the proprietor of their honeymoon vacation spot.

Opportunity knocks!

He called me explaining the situation and his idea was to send me a small cowbell, a really small one, about three inches in diameter that, when shook, went tinkle, tinkle, tinkle. He was wondering if I would attach this tiny bell to the box springs of the honeymoon bed. "Of course," I replied like a jokester in heat.

The day the honeymooners were to arrive my desk clerk, all my old maid housekeepers and I attached the tiny bell, with a small note from their best man, to the double bed farthest from the door. Newlyweds always slept (if they did) in the bed farthest from the door. Everyone, including the giggling 60-year-old maids, jumped on the bed like Olympic trampoline champions. And the bell, while muted, very clearly, tinkled, tinkled away.

The weary, but unwary, couple arrived, and we showed them to their suite for the week, all of us anxious to hear how and when they discovered the bell. The next morning — nothing. The pair was talkative, but even with prompting about how they liked their accommodations, nary a word. As far as they were concerned, everything was hunky-dory.

They left to go skiing and the maids dashed to the room convinced that they'd slept in the wrong bed. But, no, they had slept in the tinkle bed and, with inspection, the bell was still there and it still tinkled.

Three more days went by and not a murmur. They had to hear the bell so why didn't they find it or at least mention it? We were dumfounded. So was my friend from Chicago who was calling me daily.

On Thursday, I got a call from one of my Aspen friends who said he'd heard a complaint from one of my guests and thought he should report it to me.

He had been riding a chairlift with a total stranger and started a conversation:

"Beautiful day, huh?"

"Yes, it is."

"Where are you from?"

"North Shore of Chicago."

"First time in Aspen?"

"Yes, I'm here on my honeymoon. My wife wanted to do some shopping this afternoon so I'm skiing alone."

"Where are you staying?"

"We're at The Applejack Inn."

Not wanting to let the groom know that he knew me, he said, "Oh, how is it?"

"Oh, we absolutely love the place, the people are so nice and we really like the indoor pool. But we have a problem in our room."

"Oh, really?" my friend asked, "What's wrong?"

"It's the phone in the room. All night long it rings and rings and rings and, 'Hello ... Hello,' there is never anyone there."

Perfect.

P.S. I've never seen two people blush that deeply when we showed them the little cowbell attached to their bedsprings.

CHAPTER 27

Golf Carts Can Fly

Aspen was full of nuts. There were so many of them per capita that you'd swear there was a mysterious hand sprinkling them over Aspen like pecans falling from a tree.

Ted Armstrong was one of those nuts. Blond, tall and at one time lanky, but now he was just big. He had grown-up during Aspen's 1940's and 50's fledgling ski years. In the early 40's the only ski lift was a boat tow, which was a large wooden sled with 12 or so skiers aboard that was skidded, un-gloriously, up and down the lower section of Aspen Mountain. It was powered with an old, coughing, spitting, Model A Ford engine and pulled by an ancient, rusted, fraying mining cable that was rescued from a long-abandoned silver mine. But it worked and was just the ticket to get alpine skiing going in a town that needed some kind of economic shot in the arm besides potato farming.

Like so many of his era, Armstrong was full of energy and mischief and if ever there was a class clown, Ted was it. He had a constant and booming laugh that started low like distant thunder and ended high like a screech of a famished barn owl. His sense of humor was lightning fast and laced with sarcasm. He never forgot a quip and used them at every opportunity.

"Put an egg in your shoe and beat it," he'd yell at someone he hoped would leave. Like Ken Sterling, he had a derogatory and nasty nickname for everyone. Nobody escaped! There were lots of numb nuts, dumb asses and shitheads, but there were several more creative ones. The mayor was addressed as Your Boner instead of Your Honor. He called the chubby, lovable sheriff, Lon Herwick (who everyone in town called "Dirty" — behind his back of course) "Whyn't Urp." He used to say to him, "Hey Urp, see if you can find a horse strong enough to carry you and your broad-assed striped pants, and we'll rustle up a posse and go out and arrest that no-good, down easterner Sterling. And while we're at it, arrest that cute little nag he rode in on!" I was never sure if that meant Ken's wife, Martie, or an equine filly in Ken's stable — probably the former.

Teddy was the town's Director of Parks and Recreation and, to his credit, he was pretty creative in that position. He started and managed all the recreation programs for kids he could muster up. The kid's loved him and he loved being adored.

I got to know Teddy very well when he and I were opposing head coaches for the fifth and sixth grades' tackle football teams. There was no valley league so we had to scrimmage each other. With those young, skinny, wide-eyed, inexperienced players, both coaches' strategy was to pick the biggest, most aggressive kid as a linebacker and blitz him on every play. It was embarrassingly effective, but we were not teaching the kids much, so we mutually agreed to ban the blitz. As I remember it, once the blitz was gone my little team whupped his little team's collective little butts. At least that's the way I remember it and Ted is no longer around to contest it. If he were around, I might not remember it that way.

In the late 1960s Ted was also the Executive Director and Head Elite Alpine Coach for the highly esteemed Aspen Ski Club. He was a good coach with several of his protégés selected as U.S. Ski Team and Olympic team members. I was president of the club and Ted and I became quite close. Ted's coaching style focused on speed. He didn't teach the kids how to turn much but they were accustomed to going fast — very fast.

Admirably, the Aspen Ski Company ran the 1A lift for another hour after closing so the ski team kids could train on the excellent and steeper slopes of Lower Ruthies. On the last run of the evening, Ted would line the team up, ages 8 to 18, one right after another, fastest first on Dago Road, put them in their tuck and have them ski nonstop and flat out, the 10-foot-wide, hairpin-curved road all the way to the bottom.

Just skiing this road was easy, and most snowplowing neophytes use it to safely get down steep Aspen Mountain. However, at 50 to 60 miles an hour, strapped on two slats of narrow hickory, this tame road was the equivalent of racing twenty Formula One cars down and through the corkscrew of Lombard Street in San Francisco at 200 mph. The kids loved it and him.

Sometimes practical jokes come spur of the moment with no previous planning, and Ted was not one to let any opportunity pass by. One of Ted's best friends was Richard Mill. Naturally Ted called him "Dick ... Head," and he didn't mean the normal contraction of his given name. Dick was the manager of the U. S. Lumber Company down the hill on Mill Street. (Didn't dawn on me at the time, but what an appropriate street for his work!). Aspen was booming, and there was construction at every turn. The lumber business was more than thriving and vastly important to the Aspen economy.

Dick and his lovely wife, Vera, had four super kids and were pillars of family life in Aspen. Their oldest boy, Andy, was a gifted athlete who was to become one of Aspen's premiere Olympians. When Andy was young, but already recognized as a future star, Ted persuaded his good friend Dick to be president of the Aspen Ski Club. Ski racing was as important to Aspenites as the Red Sox were to the Boston bean-eaters. The Aspen Ski Club was a revered organization and to be its leader was a respected honor but also carried the responsibility of producing a string of champions. Dick was a great president and he and Ted became bosom buddies, even though their bosoms had slipped quite a bit.

Aspen had a new nine-hole golf course at the west edge of town, it was built by developer Wally Mills on a big, empty, treeless pasture that had once been the Marolt family's potato farm. The course was to be the cornerstone to a development of primary homes for the housing-starved community. The land was large enough for a full eighteen holes but Wally wanted to have saleable building lots lining the nine fairways. Surprisingly, the little course was quite nice with a pleasing visual design with lots of water, ponds and streams everywhere. The views of the surrounding snow covered 14,000-foot peaks were so spectacular it knocked not only your socks off but your shoes and knickers as well. Unfortunately for Wally but fortunately for Aspen, things didn't go as well as Wally hoped and he needed to sell the golf property. At Ted's encouragement, the city bought it and redesigned the course into a successful and respected eighteen-hole championship track.

It was on the old nine that a Ted Armstrong and Dick Mill practical joke occurred. Every year the course held the Mayor's Tournament and the City of Aspen employees were invited to play along with their guests. If not great golf, it was a good excuse to drink lots of beer, down a couple of brats and knock a ball around a bit in fall's off season. There were prizes and trophies to be won so the better golfers were competing seriously. Ted, an employee, invited his good friend "Dick...Head" to be his partner. Both had played a lot together and were competitive with each other, but as a team with lower handicaps they were to be reckoned with, and they were looking forward to victory and accepting the trophies. Just before the shotgun start, Dick splurged in the pro shop and bought a brand-new pair of expensive Titleist golf saddle shoes in sparkling white leather and brown alligator trim. He was so proud of his purchase he was a boring pest showing them all around the clubhouse, driving range and putting green. Ted, as usual, was in his dirty white tennis shoes with tied and retied broken laces and was understandably jealous.

In a new city-owned golf cart, they started out to play, full of glorious expectations. But in a two-ball format, Ted had a case of slices, and after a few holes the team was hopelessly out of the running. Dick, whose game was OK, couldn't pass up the opportunity to harp and carp and nag on the crappy play from his hapless and discouraged partner. Hole after hole this went on, and Ted sat quietly and endured it. On hole eight, I think it was, there was a midsized pond up near the green. Ted had dribbled his drive into the pond and, disgusted, drove the cart toward the edge of the lake for his drop. Dick, as passenger and with a nagging high-pitched voice, told seething Ted not to get too close to the lake as it might get his new shoes wet.

Opportunity knocks!

The pond had a small three-foot-high berm built around it. Ted, fed up with Dick's nagging, sped the cart to its limit and straight for the berm. Just at the last moment, he jumped out of the cart and it was propelled, with Dick screaming four-letter epitaphs, landing smack dap in the middle of the pond. As the cart sank slowly, Dick realized that he had on his new expensive white leather and alligator-trimmed Titleist shoes, so he took a deep breath and raised his legs as he desperately tried to hold the prized shoes out of the water.

The last thing Ted saw was the bottom of those beautiful spiked shoes disappearing slowly beneath the murky green water.

"Serves the "Dick Head" right," he roared.

CHAPTER 28
A Sign Of The Times

In the 1950s and early '60s a disastrous blight occurred in the Roaring Fork Valley. It was an eyesore that blocked out all the beautiful views of the river, the majestic peaks and pristine meadows. It was an avalanche of sorts, an avalanche of advertising billboards and signs.

Every Tom, Dick and hapless business owner in Aspen felt the need to advertise their wares along both sides of Highway 82 with thousands of signs. **Eat At Joe's Diner. Buy Skis At Acme Sports. Cozy Rooms At The Grand Hotel.** Once one lodge put up a sign, every other lodge had to have one. Then each business had to have two, then three, then twenty-four. It was an epidemic and visitors had to drive to Aspen in what was a topless tunnel of billboards.

Around 1963 a few community leaders said "enough is enough", and a campaign was initiated to get rid of the signs. Two of these leaders were medical doctors Bugsy Barnard and Jay Baxter. They recruited a young ski instructor, Norm Clasen, who had won $150 for his design of an information board at the airport where each business could have a small sign and a recorded message. This would hopefully placate the businesses that had advertised on billboards up and down the valley.

Before Bugsy would pay Norm the $150 Norm had to help the well-meaning doctors remove all the signs along the highway. Through legal and illegal channels the three of them, and others, started a "Get Rid Of All The Signs" vigilante campaign. If the business didn't agree to voluntarily remove their signs then a midnight gang of sign terrorists removed them with axe and chainsaw. Some of the businesses took exception to the pressure tactics and continued to re-erect their cut signs. Like a see saw vigilantes would lop them down again, and the owners would put them up again.

Signs soon became toxic to the community, and Pitkin County adopted a no-road-sign ordinance. Eventually it worked, and for more than 50 years the corridor between Aspen and Glenwood Springs has been clean and clear. Not a Burma Shave rhyme in sight.

You ask, "What do signs have to do with a practical joke?" Let me explain with a bit of background.

Not many people knew that Aspen's lovable Swiss restaurateur, Werner Kuster, had a partner in The Red Onion, Arnold Senn. He was also Swiss and a chef supreme. Unlike the flittering, social Werner, he rarely ventured very far from the Onion's kitchen. With one exception: Arnold had a thing for new Cadillacs and he'd venture down to Glenwood Springs to purchase a new one — every spring. While buying a new car every year was unusual, buying one and then throwing a huge party for strangers was truly rare. After he'd pick up his new Caddy, Arnold would make the rounds of all the Glenwood bars and buy everyone in the house a drink.

After a couple of years, the word spread around the Aspen drinking populace, and someone would discover the day Arnold was to pick up his car. One hundred thirsty drunks would then drive to Glenwood to partake in the free booze. Since Arnold had no special itinerary, the arid hoards would line up at the auto dealer and just tailgate the Caddy wherever it went. Bar after bar, free drink after free drink, it was a drunken party for the hangers-on and expensive for Arnold.

If he realized that his bar tabs got bigger and bigger every year, he never let on.

One spring two of those Cadillac-partying drunks were the billboard-vigilante doctors, Bugsy Barnard and Jay Baxter. More than tipsy, they were carefully winding their way back to Aspen. Halfway home, Bugsy slammed on the brakes and Jay drowsily said, "What the ... ."

His remark was cut short because there in the glaring headlights was a big ugly billboard advertising one of Aspen's businesses, a business that had refused to cooperate with the removal campaign.

Bugsy said, "That no-good sumbitch. Okay, I've got my axe in the trunk and we'll lop that son of a bitch down once and for all!" Jay laid his head back and said, "Go get 'em, Bugsy mah boy."

Bugsy was really pissed and in a fury he grabbed his trusty axe, leapt the fence, sprinted to the sign and in the dim glow of the headlights, he reared back and with a mighty Paul Bunyan heave he swung — and SPROING — the axe banged off a white-painted, six-inch-diameter steel post. His fingers, hands, forearms, elbows, shoulders, molars, eyeballs and Adam's apple were shaking like a 1906 San Francisco tremor. He was blue streak cussing and hopping around the meadow like a kangaroo in heat.

How fortunate it happeded to be the offseason because it took a good four days before Dr. Barnard felt steady enough to operate or set a broken bone.

"Young Jack Brendlinger" photo credit the author.

"Ken Sterling" photo credit the Sterling Family

"Peter Greene" photo credit author

"The Author and Better Half" Photo credit – The Author

"George Nelson" - photo credit by Author

"David 'Toiletseat' Hoff" – Photo credit – Author

"Peter and Mary Ann Greene in Costume...I Think"
Photo credit – Greene Family

"Bob George" Photo credit - George Family

"Jack Reese" Photo credit – The Author

"Joe Zanin" photo credit The Author

"Deric Hopkins" – Photo credit Hopkins Family

"John and Bette Oakes" photo credit Oakes Family

"Tony Vagnuer" photo credit Tony Vagnuer

"Don Stapleton" – Photo credit Tony Vagnuer

"Howard Englander" photo credit Howard Englander

"John McBride" photo credit the McBride Family

"Tam and Sue Scott" photo credit Scott Family

"Aspen Famous Poster" photo credit "Courtesy of Richard Allen at
www.vintageskiworld.com

"John Keleher" photo credit The Author

"Tom Anderson" photo credit The Author

"Chuck Cole" – Photo credit-Author

"Freddie Fisher" Photo Credit – "Courtesy of Sue Lum and
Barbara Lewis"

(Left to right) Al Pendorf a.k.a Fulton Begley III; Jim Furniss a.k.a. Harold Center; Marc Demmon a.k.a. Dr. Slats Cabbage. – Photo credit by Slats Cabbage, Aspen State Teachers College.

"Aspen State Teachers College Logo" Photo credit Dr. Slats Cabbage

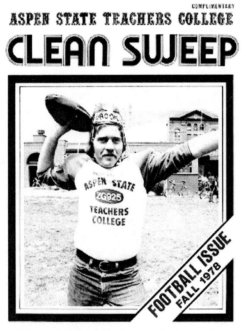

Cover of Aspen State Teachers College Newspaper"
Photo credit Dr. Slats Cabbage

"Aspen State Teachers College Beer Keg Bowling"
Photo credit Dr. Slats Cabbage

CHAPTER 29

Hey, That's My Coat and Take A Seat Please

The Hoffs, David and Ruthie, always have thrown fabulous parties and, except for the Pan Abode house on Snowbunny Lane where they lived when first married, they've always lived in custom-built, beautiful, lavish homes. One such home was high up on Red Mountain, way up on the right side of the tracks. They had an open-house party to show it off and most of the town was there, even those of us from way down there on the other side of the tracks.

Let me digress a bit to set up a couple of pranks. Dave is a former ski racer for the University of Colorado and a renowned — no, famous — powder skier who has registered more vertical miles — not feet — in the deep, deep snows served by the helicopter skiing companies of British Columbia. In the Bugaboos and Revelstoke he and Ruthie are powder snow legends. Dave is also a consummate road biker. His bikes are those very light, very expensive, made of space-age materials, and look more like a Salvador Dali painting than a usable two-wheeled conveyance.

Combining his joys of skiing and biking, Dave Hoff also has a weird fetish, he is an absolute dyed-in-the-wool equipment freak. He is known to buy eight to ten pairs of $800 skis every year in an attempt to find the perfect combination of specifications he requires. The same goes for bikes and biking accessories. Whether it's a helmet or seat, the equipment has to be a perfect fit for his big head or small ass, or his small head and big ass, I don't remember which. Never satisfied he'll keep buying and trying until he gets it right — if ever, probably never.

ꝏ 128 ꝏ

The sports manufacturers love him.

Anyway, everyone was there at the Hoff's Red Mountain Party, and a great party it was. Catered, plenty of gourmet food, and everyone was enjoying the house, the view of Aspen's twinkling lights far below, and the top-of-the-line 12-year-old single malt.

The McBrides and the Scotts had to leave early and Laurie and Sue asked Hoff where he put their coats, and Dave said he draped them over the exercise bike in the rec room. Instead of their shabby ski parkas over the exercise bike there were two gorgeous, full-length furs, one a white mink with matching muff and the other a black sable with a grey mink hood and cuffs. "Hell, why not?" the ladies thought. Dave said their coats were over the bike so these must be the right coats, and generous Dave was giving them away.

Gloriously decked out in furs, the ladies sashayed upstairs to give their thanks for a nice evening and show off the beautiful coats. Ruthie and Dave immediately recognized the fancy coats as someone else's and began to stammer as two lady guests looked alarmingly at their furs. While everybody began to protest loudly, Laurie and Sue said calmly, "But Dave gave them to us!"

During this hilarious fiasco, Marsha and I were touring the house admiring the décor and design. In a lower floor bedroom we stumbled upon a huge cardboard box the size of a waist-high steamer trunk (remember those?). The box was crammed full of barely used and brand-new bicycle seats, maybe 70 to 80 of them. No doubt a sad testimonial to Dave's equipment fetish. Since the party was winding down and guests were preparing to leave Marsha and I had an idea for a prank. We dragged that big heavy box up the stairs to the front-door landing and very formally handed a bike seat to everyone who was leaving, saying,

"David and Ruthie thank you very much for attending their housewarming party, and they want you to accept this small token of their appreciation and friendship."

AND THEY TOOK 'EM!

CHAPTER 30

Let Him Hitchhike

Ken Sterling and most of his friends loved to hunt. But put Ken anywhere near a bunch of guys he knew and a prank was sure to follow.

One autumn Ken, Dave "Toilet Seat" Hoff, Dick Parker, owner of Aspen Travel, and myself were headed out to San Luis Valley in southern Colorado to hunt ducks in the Alamosa and Monte Vista National Wildlife Refuge. We usually tried to drive over Independence Pass, the highest pass in Colorado, because it is a more direct route and would save us a hundred miles and two hours getting to the south. The pass, however, was subject to unscheduled closures because of snow, and was usually closed for the winter by late October.

It was late October but the highway department said the pass was still open so off in that direction we went. The Colorado Department of Transportation (CDOT) had a substantial metal gate on both sides of the pass, which was locked when the pass closes for the winter. We flew by the open gate on the Aspen side, drove an hour over the pass in slippery conditions, only to be shocked that the heavy gate on the other side was closed and locked by two large steel padlocks.

We weren't about to go back to Aspen and drive all the way around through Leadville when we were only a few miles from the highway heading south. However, we didn't even have a ball-peen hammer or a nail file to tackle the locks. We thought about shooting the locks with our shotguns but were pretty sure a Winchester 2¾" #4 shell wasn't going to dent the heavy metal. We also weren't too sure about where the ricochets might go.

Ken said, "Shit! Let's just build a road around that son of a bitch."

Everyone thought that was a great idea, and I immediately reminded them of my bad back and said, "I'll supervise!"

Pushing, kicking, dragging rocks and logs down the steep hillside they soon filled up the roadside ditch and in four-wheel drive we crawled over the makeshift pile to victory. CDOT be damned!

Our destination was Monte Vista, a sleepy little farming berg at the bottom of the San Luis Valley. In Spanish the name means Mountain View, and it certainly has that. There were 14,000-foot snow-topped peaks at every turn. During the duck-hunting season the two huge National Wildlife Refuges, just to the south, takes on the flavor of a war zone with everyone in camouflage, toting a shotgun and leading an overly excited black lab.

Besides hunting, the town also had another unique tourist attraction: a motel called The Movie Manor Inn. It was part of the Best Western chain as was my Applejack Inn in Aspen. I knew the owner/manager well and booked us some discounted rooms. The Movie Manor Inn was different because all their rooms had a floor-to-ceiling picture window that faced the huge screen of the local drive-in movie theater. (remember those?). Free of any additional charge, the motel piped in the sound and you could lie there and watch great movies like Steve Reeves in "Revolt of the Pigmy Slaves" or Arnold Swartzeneger in "Hercules Arm Wrestles King Kong." It was a great gimmick if you liked crappy movies and didn't like to sleep. Ken didn't and did.

He and I were roommates and since I'd stayed there before, I made sure he got the bed closest to the piped-in speakers and a perfect view of the screen. I knew the late movie they were showing had a bunch of T and A and it went on until 3 am. I also knew Ken would get hooked and watch the whole damn movie. I can sleep through anything so I said good night to Ken about 10:30 since we would be up early to hunt duck. The next morning when the alarm went off at 5 all I got from Ken was a low groan — almost a wail. Yep, as I figured, he had drunk a six-pack of Coor's Banquet and been glued to the screen until 3 and then laid awake for another hour so pissed with himself that he'd watched that whole damn crappy movie.

After breakfast, I arranged to be in the same blind with Ken because I was positive he would sleep through most of the shooting — and he did! In fact, his snoring was a pretty good "quack, quack" imitation of a sleep-starved, sex-depraved duck, and I shot my limit while he snoozed away.

Another time Ken and Dave Hoff were hunting doves with a bunch of Aspenites in La Junta, a sleepy farming community in southeastern Colorado renowned for its Rocky Ford cantaloupe and superb dove hunting. Ken and Hoff had ridden from Aspen to La Junta with Don Kopf in his new red Suburban.

Don Kopf was an Aspen character in his own right. He was always decked out in the latest and most expensive Abercrombie & Fitch hunting gear. Dressed to the nines, he considered himself the spitting image of handsome movie actor Victor Mature. In fact his friends jokingly referred to him as "Victor Mature," and I think he liked it. Ken Sterling, true to form, said he wasn't going to call him mature and tagged him with "Victor Manure," and of course it stuck.

After a day and a half of dove hunting, Ken and Hoff had shot their limit (40 birds apiece) and were anxious to start the eight-hour drive home from La Junta. However, Victor Manure still had two birds left for his limit and wouldn't leave the field even though the birds were roosting somewhere else and had stopped flying. Ken and Hoff anxiously pleaded with him, explained it would be three more hours before the birds started flying again, and they wouldn't get home until 3 am. Kopf refused to budge.

Frustrated, the two went back to the Suburban. They honked the horn continuously but no Victor Manure. So Ken said screw him, started Kopf's car and left. Hoff said, "What are you doing?" and Ken said, "I'm leaving the stubborn son of a bitch and driving back to Aspen." And he did!

Ken knew there were other Aspen groups hunting in the area and Victor Manure would be able to contact them for a ride home. If he wasn't smart enough to do that then "Let him hitchhike!"

CHAPTER 31

When is a Dove Not a Dove?

Another couple of dove stories with the same cast of characters is worthy of another chapter.

Several hunters were going to La Junta to hunt dove and they invited Dick Parker to go along. Dick was a renowned big-game hunter with a house full of African trophies so they were understandably surprised when Dick told them he'd never hunted dove and he would be delighted to go along.

When they reached the hunting site it was foggy and not a lot of doves were flying, but from the other side of the river where they had sent Dick they heard a lot of shots. A few hours later as they gathered around the cars to discuss where to hunt next, Dick arrived with a big smile and the boys said, "How'd you do?" "Got my limit," he said and proudly dumped 15 songbirds on the hood of the car. From that day on he was known as "Dicky Bird"

On another fall hunting trip Dave Hoff, Dicky Bird, Ken Sterling and Victor Manure were going over to Delta to shoot some of those dangerous attack doves, and they drove over McClure Pass in Victor's Suburban.

They had a pretty good hunt around a Delta feedlot but the dead birds always fell in the manure inside the lot and the dogs, when they went to retrieve them, happily rolled around in the muck, and the hunters were reluctant to clean both the doves and their dogs.

Back at the motel Hoff and Sterling offered to take the Suburban into town and get ice for the coolers. Manure complained, "Wait a minute, you two left me in La Junta last fall and you can't fool me twice. Give me your shotguns for collateral so I'll know you'll come back." They agreed and tootled off to Kmart.

Once in Kmart, Ken tossed the car keys to Dave and with a big shit-eating smile said, "Go get some spares made."

Now if you've read this far you know my friends are a bunch of idiots and this confirms it. Contrary to the popular saying, this group doesn't even have a top floor or an elevator to get there.

While at dinner that night, one of them said he'd heard of a town in southwestern Colorado called Dove Creek and they ought to drive down there and check it out. Any town with the name of Dove Creek must have a dump load of birds. The next day they drove 163 miles in three hours on practically nonexistent roads to discover Dove Creek was a mining town named after a local family named, you guessed it, Dove. And the townspeople had never seen a dove — ever!

They decided to stay over in Dove Creek rather than to attempt the bad road in the dark, and they would meet at the car at 6:30 and go to dinner. Hoff and Sterling, with spare keys in hand, got to the car at 6:15, opened it, started it, honked the horn until Manure looked out the window in amazement. Then they smiled, waved and drove off in a spray of mine tail dust.

Dove Creek wasn't a big town, and Sterling knew there were only a few places to eat so he let his dumbfounded friends walk, both of them praying that he hadn't gone back to Aspen.

CHAPTER 32

The Venue Makes the Difference
or Location, Location, Location

Sometimes a location lends itself as a fabulous venue for a practical joke. One such place is Heron Bay, Swan Quarter, Hyde County, North Carolina, USA.

Never heard of it, right? Not many people have, even those who've lived all their lives on the East Coast. But it is a very special place to several Aspenites, all friends of Bob George. It is a fantastic goose and duck hunting camp that has been privately owned by Bob's family since the depression years. Bob's granddad, Robert H. George, and his dad, Robert F. George, bought a few farms totaling some 800 acres just outside of the teeny, sleepy town with a great name, Swanquarter. They either paid two dollars an acre for the farms or for back taxes owed. They bought them to establish a premiere hunting camp for ducks and geese.

The farm sticks out on a point of land jutting into the southwestern shore of a freshwater, shallow lake called Mattamuskeet. The lake is a National Wildlife Refuge for hundreds of thousands of species of ducks, plus graceful, milk white swans and two kinds of geese: Canada and snow. It is major stop on the Eastern Flyway for wave after wave of migrating birds headed south for the winter. The lake, some 13 miles long, 6 miles wide and averaging 6 feet deep, is located just inside salty Pamlico Bay. This bay separates the mainland from the famous Outer Banks home of Kitty where two bicycle repairmen flew the first powered airplane. During World War II the government put huge pumps in Mattamuskeet lake and drained it to plant crops to feed the wartime eastern seaboard. The pumps, now idle, are a rusting reminder of a time when all commodities were scarce.

Pamlico Bay is also infamous because it is where Blackbeard, the pirate, would sail his schooner for sanctuary. He knew how to sail through the deeper passages, zigzagging through the treacherous shallows, some of them only a few inches deep. No pursuer would dare chase the pirate into such dangerous waters.

When the Georges bought the farm and hunting camp they needed a tenant to farm the tillable acres and plant corn and rice as an attraction for waterfowl. They hired Bruce Lee Hodges, a farmer and renowned hunting guide, who lived nearby. Bruce Lee and his wife, Vera Mae, had one girl, Ruth Lee, and four boys, Clarence, Binnie, Wayne and Timmy. The latter three were destined to be hunting guides extraordinaire.

Heron Bay is rural, really rural, Nawth Karroliina — a redneck territory with a much deeper southern feel than its proximity to the Mason Dixon Line.

The Hodges family reflects every trait you've ever heard or seen about southern rednecks. The boys are all big, NFL offensive line big. Their hands are so huge that when you try to shake hands their fingers are around your elbow. Their drawl is slower than a night crawler with a head at each end. They tend to make a one-syllable word into two, like shii'iit, or contract two words into one, like you all to y'all, or four words to one, son of a bitch to sumbitch. When they said the 'N' word (and they used to a lot, now not so much) you'd swear that word had seven syllables. They can make a simple sentence into a dissertation: "Have any of you SOBs seen my green John Deere tractor?" becomes "Haf anee y'all sumbitchs ceein mah greeein Johuun Der trahicktoor?" You need to be around them for at least a week before you can understand aneethaang.

My favorite redneck joke is about their dialect: Timmy gets pulled over by the State Patrol for driving too fast and the trooper says, "Got any I.D.?" and Timmy answers, "Bout whaat?"

Understanding them is made even worse because the brothers have lived around one another for so long they never get to, or have to, finish a sentence. The brothers have heard everything the talker has ever said about a particular subject and they just break in with their own soon-to-be-cut-short statement. When they're done, you blink your eyes and say, "Whauut?" in three syllables.

In the last few years I've noticed that their drawls are shorter and their diction more mid-America. Now that reruns of "The Beverly Hillbillies" and "Green Acres" are no longer on, it must be the influence of seven or eight hours of Oprah and Rosie on the teeveee.

Except for Binnie, who is an engineer on one of the North Carolina ferry lines, the hardy men of the Hodges' family toil nine months of the year, feeding the coffers by tirelessly farming, fishing, logging, crabbing, oystering and, of course, bullshitting every chance they get. Plus, most of their wives work and bring home a good paycheck. All this effort is just so the boys can hunt fowl and guide hunters for three months of the year.

The ways of the migratory bird is a major curlicue in their DNA passed down from granddaddy to daddy to grandson. Waterfowl is so ingrained in the clan that all the males from infant to rest home are decked out in splotchy brown camouflage 24/7 and 52 of those 7's a year. If you've read James Michener's Chesapeake, you could compare the Hodges to the Edmund Steed clan whose entire backwoods existence, generation after generation, was tied to the wonders and the hunting of the wild migratory Canada goose.

Of Heron Bay's 800 acres only 110 of them are tillable. The rest is forestry swamp — acres of dark, brackish water, only a few inches deep and full of water moccasins, black bears, possums, coons, muskrats, nutria, and tons of whitetail deer that aren't much larger than a greyhound dog. The deer are so prolific they are pests, and the locals, every man, woman and child, can bag eight of them every season.

The tillable property is crisscrossed with 8-foot-deep and 15-foot-wide canals, which are the water egress for the irrigation of the grain fields. In the spring the brothers drain the fields into the canals, plow the land and plant corn or grain for the duck's dining pleasure and for successful hunting in the early winter. Just before the hunting season, in October, they strategically set out 25 or so plywood hunter blinds, each camouflaged with dry willow branches or cornstalks. They place them in and surrounding Heron Bay's four prime hunting areas: Jerusalem, The Pond, New Pond and, best of all, The Point. When we walk into these blinds each morning, these special fields will boil with a tsunami rush of spooked ducks and geese whose numbers often reach to ten thousand. Their explosion from these flooded cornfields is incredible to your senses. Believe me, the black clouds of rising birds and the sound of thousands and thousands of beating wings are a goose-bump rush that you'll never ever forget. I never have!

Bob George had been to Heron Bay with his grandfather and father each hunting season since he was old enough to shoulder a shotgun. Before Bob unexpectedly died of a massive heart attack in 2004 he could enthrall you with fascinating tales of his indoctrination to the wary ducks and geese.

After his grandfather and father had died, Bob and his sister, Glennis, became the stewards of Heron Bay. In the mid 1980s Bob began to invite his Aspen buddies and a few other friends to join him for a week of fabulous hunting, usually right after Christmas or the first three weeks of January. So, thanks to Bob, Glennis and Bob's surviving children, Heron Bay has been an annual hunting refuge for their families and best friends for the last twenty-six years. We hunting-happy recipients were more than thankful for the opportunity.

Heron Bay is a hunter's hunting camp with two usable structures for housing, both surrounded by ramrod straight, 80-foot loblolly pines on two sides and deep, overgrown, foreboding canals on the other two. The main structure is a quaint dark brown log cabin that sleeps eight and has the only usable kitchen and bath with shower. It's main feature is a great room with an always blazing, enormous river-stone fireplace dominating one end and a huge dining table for twelve at the other. Comfortably worn chairs, stuffed sofas and ashwood rocking chairs surround a round table that serves as both card table and gun-cleaning bench. The walls and mantle are completely covered with dusty, stuffed ducks and geese, and many years' worth of collected hunting paraphernalia and memorabilia. On either side of the front door are racks and racks of very beautiful, shiny shotguns of every make and gauge. Very homey and comfortable if you're a hunter and won't miss your wife's waiting on you hand and foot for a week.

The other abode on the property is the Glass House, so called because it has a big picture window facing a bird-infested, corn-stalked, flooded field called The Pond. This is an old wooden, shingle-covered, somewhat green-painted house of undetermined age. It doesn't have running water anymore, so the Glass House is only used for overflow sleeping. After the morning hunt, tired hunters can spend the middle of the day in front of the window reading a book or watching the unbothered ducks flutter in and out of The Pond.

The very nature of waterfowl hunting lends itself to practical jokes. One joke starts every morning as hung-over hunters are rudely awakened at 4:30 by the Hodges brothers singing, "C'mon y'all, rise and shine, ya no-guud, lazy sumbitchs, dem muddafrickin duckies er tyred awaitin for ya." It's hangover disgusting but grudgingly effective! A pot is thrust at you, high-test coffee plops in a mug and slides down your throat. When the caffeine kicks in about 10 minutes later, you can't close your eyelids 'til noon. Then, in the morning foggy-breath chill, you struggle into long johns, levis, turtlenecks, two wool sweaters, two pairs of lumpy wool socks and cover it all with 20-pound camouflaged, rubber chest waders and a multilayered, down-filled hunting coat.

Once you have it all on, round as a medicine ball, you waddle out into the inky black like a penguin on Valium, using your shotgun as a tightrope walker's balancing pole.

Practical jokes and jokers are all around and you had best be on your wary toes. A few years ago, when all of us were younger and more tolerant, the mischievous Hodges boys delighted in getting each of the hunters sopping wet at some time during the week. They'd either goad them into slipping off the bouncy and icy 20-foot-long, 2-by-10 planks crossing the canals or they'd deliberately lead them into a 4-foot-deep canal that was used for irrigating the dry crops, now invisible by the flooded field.

"Here, Jack, y'all haang ona mah shoulduh, days a deep hol roun jere and I churnuf wooldn't want y'all to get ..." (splash ... cough, cough ... sputter) "... wet!" (snicker, snort) "Ah see y'all found dat sumbitch hol."

Around 10 am after the morning hunt, it was back to the cabin to pluck ducks, dry out, warm up, and stuff down a breakfast of grits, collard greens, ham hocks and 75 scrambled eggs, all deep-fried in a huge, black iron skillet full of a couple of gallons of sizzling brown lard.

There was also a mountain of Timmy's homemade cheese-stuffed flour biscuits, each the size of an Olympian's discus. Before the afternoon hunt there were about five hours to digest breakfast and sit around the great room bullshitting and getting bored. It was a great time to think up practical jokes to play against one another. No one was safe.

Old hands, hunters who'd been there before, relished plotting practical jokes on the hunters who were new to Heron Bay Camp. It was especially dangerous if you were a rookie and arriving a few days later than everyone else. It gave the predators time to plot extravagant, complicated jokes.

Poachers

One such joke, I like to call "Poachers," featured a quasi-character named Eddie Wachs. Eddie was a entrepreneur who managed businesses that were private-airplane-oriented, usually jets. He was the fixed base operator at several regional airports around the country. He was a rich, lovable horse's ass — and he knew it. Sometimes, before he got drunk, he could be a bit more than pompous. The first time he was invited to Heron Bay, he flew in his jet along with his pilot. Wachs landed over in Engelhard, rented a car and drove into the camp late at night — perfect timing for the Hodges and hunters who were already at camp and engrossed in the plot.

Timmy's wife, Jane, was the county EMT and parked the county ambulance at their trailer at the end of the dark, mile-long muddy lane, which was the only entrance to the camp. The lane was eerily overgrown with tropical brush and dense trees— a spooky canopy over any vehicle. The plan was to allow Eddie's rental car to enter the dark driveway and Jane's ambulance, which was ready, would pull in behind him with siren blaring and red lights flashing. The ambulance had ultra-bright headlights and hand-directed spotlights blinding Eddie and blocking the fact that it was an ambulance and not a squad car. Eddie's car stopped and patriarch Bruce Hodges, his huge son

Wayne and lanky Aspenite John Keleher surrounded the vehicle. All were wearing official deputy sheriff's badges, side arms and cradling menacing double-barreled shotguns. In a sharp commanding tone, Bruce demanded that Eddie and his pilot get out of the car and spread eagle over the hood. Eddie, flustered but still obstinate, resisted, and the "officers" weren't shy about forcing him over the fender and roughly handcuffing him. In their best Deliverance drawl they gruffly demanded that he tell them what the hell he was doing on a deserted back road in the middle of the night.

Eddie said meekly, "I'm on my way to a hunting camp I thought was down this road."

"Huntin' camp? Y'all mean to tell me, Boy, y'all got guns and ammo in this here car. Did ya know, Boy, that it's agin the law in Hyde County to transport firuh arms without a transportation parmit? Ya gots a parmit, Boy?"

"Uh, uh, no, I... I didn't know."

"Ignorunce is no xcus, Boy. What y'all plannin' to do with dem arms, Boy? Rob sum sumbitch?"

"No, I... er... we are going to hunt ducks and geese at Bob George's Heron Bay Camp."

"Aha! Did ju heer that, boys, that stinkin' George place is the one we'all ar accusin of poachin geese and shootin after hours." We gonna catch dos sumbitches sum ... ,"

Eddie started, "No, no, Bob is a very honest......."

Eddie's sentence was cut short by a very loud shotgun blast ... KABOOM ... from in the trees. Shocked, Eddie began to whimper when a few seconds later a very dead 15-pound goose plunked onto the hood of the rental car.

Laughter erupted from the black woods and all the hidden hunters and the fake cops roared. Rookie Eddie was officially indoctrinated.

Poachers II

A few years later, when my son Kurt, fresh out of UCLA film school, arrived late at camp, we reprised the Poachers joke. Since he was young and vulnerable, the frightening, menacing "deputies," Timmy and Wayne, had him unload all his luggage, and they searched all his belongings, dumping everything on the road and admiring his Y-front jockey shorts, "Ooooeee, Boy, lookey heer at these nice bloomers!" They confiscated his gun and threatened to haul him to the pokey unless he paid an enormous fine on the spot. He obviously didn't have that kind of money, and he stammered, stuttered and was getting noticeably stressed. Stepping out into the lights, I yelled, "CUT! This scene just isn't working. We need to do another take." Kurt, weak-kneed and checking his shorts, was still gasping and admitted all he could think of was Deliverance and he was about to bolt for his life. Good thing he didn't, because there were deep ditches, on both sides of the car, filled with murky water and water moccasins.

Kurt, like his father, didn't get mad but he liked to get even. That trip there were several other sons in camp: Robbie George, Bob's son, and Carter Schlumberger, Cowboy Marty's son, all of them full of piss and vinegar. Kurt, always the ringleader, conned the other boys into a couple of get-even jokes to play on Timmy.

The pluckin' house was a small white shed behind the log cabin. There is no door on the shed and inside was a low wooden bench along three walls where all the hunters would sit with gunnysacks over their laps and pluck all the ducks and geese shot that morning or afternoon. Standing outside listening to the banter, you'd think there was more bullshit in the pluckin' house than feathers. After several weeks of the season, hundreds of birds had been stripped, and the pluckin' house would be waist deep in down and feathers.

One evening when all the hunters were lazing around the fire, Kurt and his gang stuffed the cab, floorboards to headliner, of Timmy's pickup with all the stinky feathers from the pluckin' house. They knew

Timmy had to drive a mile or so to get home and they relished that he'd have to remove, by hand, all those feathers before he could drive.

Not all things work out as you plan. Timmy came out and with a tipsy, grinning snarl jumped in the cab, opened both doors, sped off down the road and the wind sucked out every last little feather. Damn! On to the next Get Even!

The Case of the Missing Trawler

I call this Get Even, "The Case of the Missing Trawler." Timmy and his brother, Wayne, had big oceangoing fishing boats they used for gill net fishing, crab-potting and oyster-raking. These weren't run-abouts, they were long and deep with wheelhouses and big powerful inboard diesel engines. They were docked in a small saltwater slough that had direct access to the bay and sea. Like most farms tons of equipment are all over the yards, around the farmhouse and barns. Around Timmy and Jane's house and barns there was so much equipment you couldn't see the yard. Some of it had died long, long ago and were cobwebbed sentinels to a time gone by. Newer equipment and tools could be coaxed into a useful life, like an old but functional 2-ton tandem-wheeled, flatbed truck that had one of those long ball-bearing rollers across the back to roll off heavy loads.

Kurt's gang surreptitiously fired it up. Oh joy! But how could they use it for a Get Even on Timmy? I don't know who thought of it or how they ever imagined they could pull it off. They decided to take the truck to Timmy and Wayne's dock and see if they could haul Timmy's huge fishing trawler out of the slough and onto the truck. Using the cover of darkness, they somehow winched that boat onto the flatbed and slowly, with trepidation, hauled that prize some 15 miles back to the camp and offloaded it into the New Pond hunting field.

The water in the New Pond was only 20 inches deep, and the big ole boat settled into the shallow water and with a creaking sigh laid over to starboard about 40 degrees. If ever there was a bloated whale on a beach, this grounded boat was it. The Get Timmy Gang knew that we would be hunting either Jerusalem or The Pond in the afternoon and that Timmy couldn't miss seeing the big white tub abandoned there for all the hunters to giggle at.

What they didn't count on was that Timmy's brother, Wayne, was up very early and went out in his boat to clear his gill nets of speckled trout. At the hunt that morning Wayne asked Timmy what the hell had he done with his boat. Timmy, somewhat baffled and thinking Wayne was pulling his leg, said,

"Nuttin, sheez still dere — dere ware sheez always been."

"Uh-uh," Wayne insisted, "Ahm not kiddin, that sucker ain't there. Sum sumbitch dun stol y'all's boaat!"

This conversation went on all morning and after the morning hunt, Timmy reluctantly left to check it out. The boat was gone — but before he reported it as stolen he thought, ooh yeah, them nasty lil basturds are pullin a lil ole joke on me.

Timmy knows everyone in the county so he called a close friend who was a real deputy sheriff and asked him to stop by and question the boys. The deputy played his part well and while the boys didn't own up to anything, he could tell there was guilt in the air.

On the way to New Pond that afternoon, all the in-on-the-joke hunters were riding in the back of Timmy's truck and joyously anticipating his reaction. But being typically Timmy, who may have been shocked to see his beached boat in the pond, totally ignored it — pissing everyone off, especially the boys. Plus, getting the boat out of The Pond onto the truck and back to the dock was a lot harder than vice versa, and a lot less fun for the "Missing Trawler Gang."

What Time Does Your Watch Say?

Another elaborate joke was pulled on newcomers Tom Schroeder and Brad Zanin. I've named this one "What time does your watch say?" All the other hunters planned a creative stunt to welcome these neophytes. Jack Reese (see patsy in the next story) noticed Brad didn't wear a watch and when Tom took a shower just before going to bed, Reese reset Tom's watch ahead three hours. Normally everyone gets up at 4:59 a.m. to be in the blinds just before sunrise. After the rookies hit the sack, we snuck around and set all the wall clocks ahead three hours. At 2 am the Hodges woke everyone and told us to get dressed and be ready to hit the blinds. All the hunters were in on the gag, got dressed and followed Wayne and the unsuspecting marks out to the pitch-black fields and pretended to go to their selected blinds.

Wayne took the "pigeons" to a remote blind and told them to cover the water directly in front of them when the sun rose — and he left. Filled with anticipation, the hapless hunters waited patiently for sunrise. Little did they know that the dawn was still three hours away. The rest of the giggling hunters had gone back to the cabin, undressed and, still snickering, slept for another two-and-a-half hours.

My Bed Is Realy Lumpy, How's Yours?

This joke is called, "My bed's really lumpy, how's yours?" Two of Bob's closest Aspen friends, Jack Reese, a witty jokester in his own right, and Joe Zanin, a great storyteller, were finally invited, and, from all they'd heard about what a great a hunting camp Heron Bay was, they were both very excited to get there. However, they were rookies and the old-timers would be waiting for them, not with open arms but with a creative practical joke.

I've already described the accommodations, rustic but very comfortable. However, on the property down a rutty bouncy road, more a weedy path than a road, was an old dilapidated cabin. The cabin was used to house an old black man named Clem, who for years was the handyman around the farm. To hear the Hodges tell it, Clem was also the best damn goose-duck-swan-pluckin sumbitch in the entire South. He's gone now, but the stories of his pluckin linger on. I'm told he could pluck three geese in the time it took one of the Hodges to pluck a tiny blue-winged teal.

After Clem died there was no one to live in his one-room shack with a one-holer outback, and the Hodges had let it go to seed. The windows were cracked or gone. The faded wallpaper was peeling away from the wall next to the door and window frames. In several spots the bare wood floor was curling up like kinky wet hair. The posts under the small front porch had rotted away and it slanted jauntily to the east while the rest of the structure leaned to the west.

Realizing that the best of jokes take some preparation, Bob and the plotting hunters were delighted to spend a whole afternoon trying to make the dump somewhat presentable. They put curtains over the empty window frames and hauled in two army cots and made them up with fresh sheets, pillows and fuzzy, two-toned Hudson Bay wool blankets. They found a rickety old table, put a cloth on it and topped it with a Coleman kerosene lantern and a pitcher of lemonade with two glasses. For chairs they installed two pretty good-looking Ducks Unlimited rockers. The decorators were pleased. The place was still a dump, but in the twilight it passed as almost livable — especially when your cordial host dropped you and your luggage off, lied to you that this was it, and after you were unpacked you should come to dinner at 7, and then drove off. Bob had also rigged a hidden camera so he could record the new arrivals' reactions.

Jack and Joe didn't say anything for a few minutes, just looked around dumbfounded. They sat in the rockers, didn't say much, just sat there, not rocking, in gaped-mouthed awe. Joe broke the ice, got up and went over to the cot and sat on it, squirmed a bit and said, "My bed's a bit lumpy, how's yours?" Then, both talking at once, they got serious about the state of their accommodations. "Do you think this is what it's like here? It seems a bit ... er... rustic."

"I don't know, but I don't think there's any glass in these windows. I'm sure it gets cold at night."

"Do you see any stove or fireplace or anything for heat?"

"I gotta go! Did I see an outhouse in the back?

"Joe, I...I don't think I can stay here, it won't be good for my asthma!"

"Mine either," Joe admitted, taking a long hit on his breathalizer. "But how do we tell Bob that we have to move to a motel?"

"I've heard there are no motels for miles. What are we going to do? We're here for a week!"

In unison: "Shiiiitt!"

Gotcha, boys. Y'all come on up to the main cabin where it's warm and cozy! Ya hear?

CHAPTER 33

Deric Hopkins, Pyromaniac

It is a good thing the military destroyed all the M9A1-7 flamethrowers used in Vietnam because if they were available Deric Hopkins would own two or three and use them to scare the crap out of all his friends and enemies.

For most of us normal people, innocuous fireworks at the Fourth of July picnic that fissile and spark some two feet high is enough pyrotechnics to last us for a year. But wannabe firefighter Deric just can't get enough of the hiss, boom and bang stuff.

Deric and his wife Pam and their lovable family; Brett, Shawn and Julie moved to Aspen in 1967 when Deric was hired to financially advise an old friend, Chuck Hall. The attractive, outgoing, personable and fun-loving Hopkins were an immediate and welcomed addition to

Aspen's rapidly growing family contingent.

Aspen was and is a party town. The tourists, or "Turkeys" as the locals endearingly used to call them because they started showing up at Thanksgiving, loved Aspen for its myriad of superb restaurants and nightlife. Come Friday and Saturday nights the locals also did their damndest to let their hair down and party on in those same establishments.

Every weekend, one of the locals would stage a party and invite all the young Aspenites over for a dinner, buffet or potluck and serve mandatory cocktails, most of the time BYOB. Usually that was not enough to guarantee a good case of the "Brendlinger flu" the next morning, so we'd all go out to The Tippler to dance to the Walt Smith Trio or to The Night Club in the basement of the Golden Horn just to dance, drink and laugh.

Deric couldn't wait to be invited or not invited to a party so that he would have the excuse to light off his pyrotechnics. Bottle rockets, string of firecrackers, cherry bombs, roman candles and aerial bombs were his specialty. He'd set them off near the front and/or backdoor of the house — anywhere they would be loud enough to disrupt the party. One night he saw the smoke coming from the chimney of a party house where he hadn't been invited, even though he knew nearly everyone there. He got a ladder, climbed on the roof and dumped several firecrackers in the chimney.

Many a time he would just wait until everyone was in bed and at 3 am set off his grandiose and loud display, waking everyone in the house and most of the hood.

Marsha and Jack Reese's wife, Beverly, were great party-givers, and they always gave spectacular creative parties for their pair of Jacks' major birthdays. Reese's is in late January and mine a few days later in February. For our fortieth, they threw a sit-down formal dinner at Maurice's in the Aspen Alps. It was a grand affair and Jack and I were honored and enjoying it immensely. That is until our friends Anderson,

Hopkins and Zanin presented Reese with a birthday gift, a box the size of a small trunk. When Jack started to take the wrapping off, the box moved.

Jack jumped back and announced, "I'm not touching that damn thing." When he was finally convinced it wasn't dangerous, he carefully opened it and out popped a greased piglet. A donnybrook ensued as everyone tried to catch the frightened pig as it scampered throughout the restaurant, scaring wives, waiters, bartenders and an alarmed restaurant proprietor, Maurice, who was leaping around screaming French epitaphs that I'm sure would make Bonaparte blush

The practical jokers had only borrowed the piglet from a local farmer, and Reese and another guest, Don Westerlind, knew it had to be returned early in the morning, so they turned the tables on the jokers.

Reese and Westerlind took the captured piglet to the Aspen Police Department, left it there with the information that it had been stolen and the thieves had lost it and would come to the station to retrieve their stolen property, and the police should arrest them.

Back to Hopkins! For the pair of Jacks' (takes two queens to beat us) fiftieth birthday party, Marsha and Beverly booked the Diamond J Guest Ranch up in the Frying Pan River Valley beyond Ruedi Dam. It was a famous old dude ranch that had been popular for decades and decades. The structures on the ranch included a two-story main lodge with conference and party space and several guestrooms, plus several outbuildings, consisting of very nicely appointed housing space and barns and corrals — All of them constructed with old dried-out logs and, naturally, very flammable.

We knew there would be a tad bit of drinking so we booked overnight accommodations so no one had to drive back to Aspen. It was wintertime and there was beautiful, deep Colorado snow all over the ranch and the surrounding mountains. We were there to enjoy the cross-country skiing, which we did before the evening birthday banquet. It was a great party with heaps of barbecue beef, ribs, chicken, baked beans, buttered corn and mounds of steaming cornpone bread— washed down by lots of alcohol.

The roasting of the two Jacks was hilarious. Eventually, some revelers tried to go to bed early but none of us would have that and rescued them from their cozy beds to join us in the outdoor, oversized hot spa. There were several couples enjoying the 104-degree water and soothing jets — everyone but Deric. Where was he? Suddenly there was a huge fireworks display not far from the tub. The drunks were cheering, clapping and screaming, "Yea, Deric." But, it wasn't over. There was Deric with an armload of Roman candles, giggling while he lit and aimed them at all of us in the spa. With red, green and blue fireballs flying everywhere, we timed it and, in unison, all ducked under the water, easily avoiding the menacing missiles. Thankfully, no one got burned nor, luckily, did we set fire to the tinder-dry ranch. The only damage was catastrophic onslaught of the dreaded Brendlinger flu the next morning.

A few years later Bob George and I were on a mountain rescue in the same area of the Frying Pan Valley, and the proprietor of the Diamond J Ranch was the attending EMT. Unfortunately, she recognized us and relentlessly scolded us, saying we were the worst guests they had ever had up to that time — and since!

We were red-faced embarrassed, but it also brought up fond memories of how much fun we had up to that time — and since.

CHAPTER 34

If It's Rainy Out, Don't
Leave It Out

If you need a leader, someone to masterfully run your fundraiser, or organize a treacherous mountain rescue at 3 am in the middle of a blustery winter storm, or step up to lead the band down Main, Bob George was your man!

As a teenager Bob was transplanted to Aspen from Bradford, Pa. Luckily for the town, his parents decided to leave Pennsylvania and make Aspen their home. Bob was a friendly Huck Finnish good-looking kid whose engaging personality endeared him immediately to the cliquish Aspen school kids. Early on he showed masterful abilities in organizing his friends for a prom, a kegger or a hunting trip.

He went to the University of Colorado and met his future wife Karen there. Settling in Aspen, they had three children and Bob became the manager and later co-owner of Aspen's number-one real estate business, Mason and Morse.

He was organized. His office at work was a work of art, nothing out of place. Even if you could find a speck of dust, it looked like it belonged there. As if he were playing a practical joke on his family, his personal office at home, however, was a living, breathing mess. Stacks and stacks of books and papers were everywhere, covering his desk (if you could find it), floor, bookcases, even on the TV, piled higher than the rabbit ears. It totally defied the town's image of the man.

Whether it was in Heron Bay, his prized hunting camp in North Carolina or on the streets of Aspen, Bob George was full of mischief and he delighted in displaying it wherever he was and whenever he could. Like New York City!

Every year in late October New York City puts on a premier marathon where tens of thousands of nuts show off their craziness to run, jog, walk or crawl 26.2 grueling miles. They trot on filthy, hard, hot, black pavement in front of hundreds of thousands of screaming spectators, half of them homeless and half with one shoe sole that flaps. Why in any consciousness would anyone run 26.2 miles? For you runners whose elevator doesn't get to the top floor, you always answer, "Because it's good for you!" Huh?

Just thinking about participating in a marathon is hard enough, but you have to train for six months, running every day, sometimes as much as 20 to 22 miles just for the opportunity to say you can do it. Hah! The Aspen orthopedic surgeons are the only ones who think, "Because it's good for us!"

Several Aspen ladies, Karen George, Janny Anderson, Connie Nostdahl and Marsha Brendlinger, took up running for exercise. Frankly, I think they did it so they all could simultaneously talk at one another as they jogged along. Some fitness guru told them a good marathon pace was one you could carry on a natural conversation without gasping or wheezing. The ladies minded that advice and ran at a two-miles-per-hour pace but talked at a 20-miles-per-hour rate. Their chattering was so speedy and constant I don't know how anyone listened. I guess it was just an opportunity to tell everyone else what was on your heaving, gasping chest. Most every day they would see another more dedicated male runner who would ask them as he passed, "How far are you ladies going to talk today?"

As their sentences got more compound and the miles longer, they decided to train for a marathon. "Why not? I'm sure we all can talk for 26.2 miles. Piece of cake!"

Several runners in ultra-health-conscience Aspen decided to run the New York Marathon in 1984, the same year the ladies targeted. The men who planned to run, to name just a few, were Don Stapleton,

Magne Nostdahl, Barry Mink, Mac McGinness. The race was to be inundated with sweaty Aspenites.

As a marketing executive with the Aspen Skiing Corp, I had been traveling all over the eastern seaboard drumming up business, and my favorite hotel in Manhattan was the historic Algonquin. It was old and funky but since it had been the home of the Algonquin Round Table, where several famous writers and theatrical icons (Robert Benchley, Heywood Broun, Harold Ross, Alexander Woollcott, George S. Kaufman and Dorothy Parker) met daily, it had more than a touch of class. Most important, for me anyway, its cozy walnut-walled bar offered up a famous large, gin martini — neat, of course.

On one trip I had to stay over an extra night and usually that is not a problem for a city hotel as they have about a 25 percent no-show rate. However, the Algonquin was booked solid with a convention group, and they asked if I would mind moving across the street to the two-star Royalton and they would pay the bill. I said fine and checked in. Surprisingly, the room had been recently redecorated, was very clean and comfortable, and at a rate of $55 a night was a steal in the Big Apple where the average room rate in 1984 was in the low to mid $100s. I stayed there a few more times and for the price thought it was fantastic. A real find!

When the marathoners, spouses and other hangers-on asked my opinion on city accommodations, I said with Brendinger' bravada, "No sweat, count on me! I'll make all the reservations — you're going to love it!"

I called The Royalton and said I wanted to reserve seven rooms on the fifth floor, where I knew all the rooms had been redecorated. I was assured it would be as I requested. We arrived and I was anxious to show off my expertise. WRONG! Only two of the seven were on the fifth floor; the others were spread around. I complained and they said they were sorry but they had upgraded us to their suite rooms.

Marsha and I were staying on the fourth floor and, stepping off the clanking elevator, I knew I was in deep doo-doo. The carpet in the long hall was so loose it made a series of foot-high waves reminding me of "surf's up" in Malibu. The suite was all of that because it had two huge soccer-field-size rooms, one the bedroom and the other a sitting room the size of a convention hall, and there was an enormous bath to match. The carpet was multicolored, not woven that way, but because of decades of stains of dubious origin. The mohair couch and matching chairs were bald and had dandruff. Both were overstuffed and leaking. Even the doilies on their arms were tattered and gray. The bath floor had little white mosaic tile all lined up like desks in a classroom but several of them were playing hooky and the maintenance man had troweled in some sort of gray mastic to fill the gaps and color match the doilies in the arena. There was no shower and, of course, the rusty mineral-stained tub rested on little rusty feet that looked like cougar paws. A tour of the suite promised that Marsha was going to hate The Royalton, hate me, and hate the rest of the neighborhood.

Actually, everyone thought the place was a hilarious practical joke I had played and of course I didn't tell them anything different. Drinking cocktails out of Budweiser beer cups, we all sat around in one of the coliseums amusing one another on how "our joke of a room" was worse than "your joke of a room." The two couples on the redecorated fifth floor felt left out of the fun.

We non-racers had booked a limo to take the runners to the race start at the Staten Island Verrazano Bridge. After leaving the incredible mass of runners, we asked the limo driver if he knew the entire race route through the five boroughs and if there were any bars where we could sit and watch our wives run by? He did.

True to non-running-spouse form, we traveled from bar to bar along the route toasting and cheering our tiring better halves on to victory. Actually, the weather was horrendous for a race, even for a trot around a park bench. The temperature was 95 degrees with 98 percent humidity. The racers were so hot the organizers ran out of water and one runner died. Marsha, bless her and her good-for-your health mentality, finished — barely. She was suffering from acute dehydration and spent several nail-biting hours wrapped up in a space blanket recuperating in an overcrowded, makeshift Central Park infirmary.

A celebration party and a good night's sleep recharged everyone, and all were hot to sightsee Manhattan the next morning. We did all the tourist attractions: MOMA, Guggenheim and the Met art museums, the Empire State Building and more. For dinner that night I assured everyone, although most were skeptical, that I knew a perfect place and had made reservations for all of us. It was my favorite restaurant in New York City. It was in West Village and named Marguerite's, an atmospheric Italian restaurant and a hangout for opera singers who performed a constant stream of popular arias to entertain the diners.

Our reservations were also on Halloween night when the Village goes wild and most of the in-the-know New Yorkers stay away from the Village like a cobra avoids a mongoose convention. But we weren't in-the-know and wanted to experience it all. Most of our group hadn't been to the city in some time, if ever, and were ignorant of changes in the Village by the influx of the gay community.

Four couples, the Georges, the Nostdahls, the Kelehers and the Brendlingers, caught the subway a couple of hours before our dinner reservations, allowing us time to see the elaborate costuming and the notorious gay/lesbian Halloween parade in Columbus Square. We squirreled our way up to the parade barricades for unobstructed viewing. The costumes were as outlandish and as creative as any we'd ever seen. Most were a lot of transvestites dressed exquisitely as Cinderella, Queen Mary, Bo Peep, and one was riding a papier-mâché horse and claimed to be a very hairy Lady Godiva. I was afraid to look. Linda Keleher thought they all looked "divine" and told them so. Working the parade was a young chubby policeman standing on the other side of the barricade from us, and after a few minutes of numerous Cinderellas jiggling his rosy cheeks, he ducked under to our side saying, "Whew, it's a lot safer over here."

After a great dinner of scrumptious Parmesaned everything and entertained by beautiful operatic singing, we left the restaurant in a misty rain and everyone slipped on their raincoats. Most had rain jackets but Bob George had on a three-quarter-length tan London Fog overcoat, popular with flashers.

Linda Keleher had come to New York with the runners, not because she wanted to see the race, but because she didn't want to miss the shopping! Linda was a consummate shopper. Sated with ravioli and Chianti, our group strolled toward the corner to catch a couple of cabs for Uptown, but Linda noticed a shop that was open and had a long line in front of it. "Ohhh! Let's go see why that shop is so popular." The girls got in line and the boys sidled up to see what the shop was selling. We nudged each other. It was a porno shop! We let the girls wait in line until they were at the door and then we told them. Without a blink they all chimed, "Well, we've never been in one so it's high time we go and see what all the excitement is about."

We men gulped but followed our wives into the packed store. It was a first-class porno shop — if there is such a thing. Freshly painted white walls were lined with descriptive magazines discreetly hidden behind nearly opaque plastic that masked the nasty covers. The center of the large room was dominated by gorgeous, sparkling glass, antique display cases that would be more at home in Tiffany's on Fifth Avenue. However, in this shop, the contents were not diamond tiaras and necklaces but every kind of sexual aid and mechanism imaginable — totally incongruous to the classy cases.

We were surprised and a bit embarrassed by the interest of our ladies. To us they seemed to be taking an unexplainable interest in the dildo section with everything from knobby and filigree protrusions to ultra-long members with hand cranks. Finally satisfied (perhaps a poor choice of words), the ladies said, "Let's go, we've seen enough!" The men thought, "Great, at least they didn't buy anything —even the stuff on sale!"

Outside it had stopped raining but was chilly, so we kept our coats on. We ambled toward the corner and, trailing us, Bob George sidled over to walk beside Linda.

"Pssst, Linda," he whispered, "I've got a confession to make but you can't tell anyone, OK?"

Always one to help, Linda said, "It's OK, Bob, your secret is safe with me. What's the problem?"

He replied pleadingly, "Well, since I was a little kid I've had an un-controllable case of psychiatric kleptomania. When I'm in a store I just have to take something. I just can't help it! Here, let me show you," and he picked up her hand and put it on the pocket of his raincoat.

Linda screamed, "Oh my God, Bob!" "SCREEEAM"

She was in a full backward run and passed us still yelling and point-ing at Bob.

All of us turned to see Bob grinning, his arms spread wide with palms up. Obviously he was proud of himself.

"What in the world did you do to Linda?" we blurted.

"Nothing!" he claimed, shrugging his shoulders. "I just put her hand on my raincoat pocket so she could feel the fold-up umbrella in there

CHAPTER 35

OWEEE! OWEEE! OWEEE!

J im Chesley was Aspen's outdoor playboy. If there was a hunting, fishing, kayaking, climbing, hiking or camping toy to play with, he had it and used it. In the early 1960s Tom Fleck and Jim owned The Abbey restaurant, a superb prime rib/steakhouse on the alley right in the middle of town behind Long's Drugstore and across from the first-floor Elks Club and Tom's Market. Jim was probably the main reason I bought a piece of property and built a lodge in Aspen. He was a CU fraternity brother and had been after me for some time to get to Aspen and get in on the boom. I'm grateful he did.

The Abbey was a charming small restaurant with a balcony and decorated with beautiful Victorian stained-glass windows. Its main fare was a one-and-a-half-inch thick slice of juicy rare prime rib beef, a fat baked potato and a Caesar salad on the side. Yum! It also had a cozy nightclub in the basement featuring a series of excellent guitar-strumming folksingers. They entertained the late-night crowd from a minute stage in front of a floor–to-ceiling backlit stained-glass window. The club was very popular and always crowded with the folksy headband crowd.

When Jim and Tom bought the restaurant, Jim decided that their heavyset chef, Norm, might not show up some night and Jim better learn the ins and outs of the kitchen — just to be safe. I think Norm sort of resented the non-confidence in him and decided to play a joke on this kitchen neophyte.

Jim showed up midmorning as Norm was preparing the prime ribs for broiling and wrapping the potatoes in foil for baking later. Jim was observing but he was also writing everything down!

Find an apron, turn on broiler, take meat from walk-in, set it on the left side of counter, wipe hands on apron, check to see if broiler is on, wipe hands on apron, find lettuce and so on.

It was driving Norm nuts. "Jim, go home and come back at 4:30 and we'll prepare the dinners together, OK?" "Right!"

Jim was back at 4:30, anxious to learn. Diners arrived and Norm instructed, "Just watch a few times and do what I do, OK" "Right!" Jim got out his notebook. Norm checked order tickets, sliced a medium-rare, slice of steaming meat, placed it on a large dinner platter, spooned up a healthy portion of salad, reached in the oven for a large foil-wrapped baked potato, sliced it open and garnished it with butter, sour cream and chives. Jim wrote furiously. Norm checked more tickets, went through the routine a few more times and, smiling, he turned to Jim and said, "Got it?" "Yeah, piece of cake."

Checking his notes, Jim did everything confidently and perfectly

—— up to the baked potato. Norm had reached in and grabbed a potato with his bare hand, not explaining that after 40 years of cooking potatoes his hands were so callused he could pick up a red-hot coal and feel nothing. With his bare hand Jim reached in the oven for a foiled potato and instead of it dropping on the plate, it stuck to his hand and he hopped around screaming OWEEE! OWEEE! OWEEE! trying unsuccessfully to shake it loose. Biting his lip, Norm stuck Jim's hand, still holding the hot potato, in a bucket of ice he had prepared for just such an occasion.

Even after he'd bought some tongs, it took several weeks before a wary Jim attempted to help Norm again.

CHAPTER 36

C'mon, Man, Let Me Carry That

Since Jim Chesley, co-owner of The Abby restaurant, worked nights he was always trying to get his friends to join him on his daytime adventures or misadventures. He was an outdoor playboy. Whatever outside activity was new, he bought the equipment, taught himself how to use it, then hounded his friends to join him. He pissed me off because he was so damned good at whatever he tackled, rock-climbing, kayaking, spelunking, fly-fishing, bow-hunting — it didn't matter. I've got a million stories about our misadventures, like the time we were climbing on the cliffs above the Grottos and almost crushed a speeding Jag on Independence Pass when we shoved a big, teetering and dangerous rock off the mountain, or the time I got stuck upside down in a kayak in the Applejack swimming pool while he was teaching me to roll, or the time we were bow-hunting on Richmond Hill and an enormous seven-point bull elk charged us because he was mad we weren't the bull he'd been challenging, or the time we were caught above timberline on Hayden Peak in a freak blinding snowstorm in little more than T-shirts.

No matter what he proposed, parachuting behind a jeep, tubing in whitewater, or climbing a Fourteener, he always had a willing patsy: me. It's a good thing that Marsha thought I was safe behind the Applejack front desk most of the time.

Every August Jim led us on a backpacking-fishing-Cclimbing trip to the wild Pierre Lakes, located above timberline in a huge moonlike valley between Capital Peak and Snowmass Peak. It's a difficult nine-mile hike, part of it up the middle of a waterfall and then scrambling over hundreds of huge boulders the size of an army barracks. Even without a heavy pack the trip would be exhausting. We each carried about 55 pounds in our backpacks, enough goodies to stay out three nights, gear to catch 18-to-22-inch cutthroats, Wylers' Grape Juice spiked with 120-proof grain alcohol, and equipment to climb the imposing 14,000-foot Capitol Peak.

To reach the nearly vertical peak you had to negotiate the infamous Knife Edge, a ridge so narrow you had to sit down straddling the sharp, craggy edge and skinny for about 45 yards with 3,000 feet of vertical exposure beneath each leg. Gulp! Once Jim and I were roped together, and I, being in the position to belay should he fall said, "Wait a minute, if you fall off how do I belay you?" He said, without hesitating, "You jump off the other side." That was Jim — always the joker, maybe.

A group of us went to Pierre Lakes for nearly ten years and then knee infirmities began to catch up with us older adventurers. On my last trip I was accompanied by Jack Reese, Stan Jensen, Chuck Cole and Skip Behrhorst, a young in-shape whippersnapper about 15 years younger than any of us.

It was our custom to meet on Thursday night with all our gear and

supplies and divvy up everything, using a scale so that we were all carrying equally weighted packs. Skip showed up, dropped off his gear,
and excused himself as his wife had him booked elsewhere. Would we
pack his pack for him? No problem, Skipper, we really nice guys will
pack it all up. We divided everything at about 55 pounds apiece, then
the three of us looked at each other, thought about how old we were
and how young and healthy Skip was, and, to even things out a wee bit,
we put a 30 pound rock in the bottom of his pack.

We were scheduled to leave right after work on Friday, and when
we picked up Skip we urged him to get going so he didn't have time
to think about his heavy pack. . He was struggling just to raise it to his
shoulders as we bit our lips.

He began to lag behind as soon as we hit the trail, and didn't
understand why we old farts had so much bounce in our steps. We,
of course, ribbed him about his slow pace every chance we got. We
would usually walk four-and-a-half steep miles to the bottom of the
waterfall and stay there overnight. At the waterfall we were sure Skip
would discover the rock, but he didn't and just kept remarking how
spry we were and how sluggish he was. We said it must be the altitude.

The next morning we got up early, struggled to climb through the
waterfall and scrambled over the big, rugged boulders to get to the
largest, fishable Pierre Lake about noon — in time to set up a nice
camp and catch our dinner. Skip struggled over the rocks like a blind
three-legged turtle as we jeered, "Hey, Skip, c'mon man, it's obvious
you're not in good enough shape for this trip. Let us carry that pack
for you!"

At the lake he found his hitchhiking rock. I'm not sure he's ever
forgiven us.

CHAPTER 37

God Must Have Missed a Putt!

Golfing in Aspen or Snowmass was very easy back in the late 1960s and early '70s. Both areas had relatively new golf courses and most of the residents were either too busy or too lazy to take up the game. You could walk on for a tee time anytime you wanted. I had started playing golf in Denver when I was sixteen. I had a nighttime job and lots of daytime hours to devote to this difficult game. I was hooked like a bad vaudeville act. Throughout the ensuing years I made sure I found the time to play a few rounds, no matter where I was.

In Aspen, I had a great assistant manager at the Applejack and I was able to play nine holes three or four times a week. Certainly more often than my wife, Marsha, knew or suspected. My handicap hovered around a five and the better players in town were seeking me as a partner or at least didn't say "no" when I asked to play with them.

Heiko Kuhn, son of a German merchant ship captain, was a U.S. Army 10th Mountain Division trooper during the World War II campaign against the Nazis in the mountains of Italy. He was a muleskinner and was wounded during that action. He was a superb basketball coach for Leadville High and led them to three consecutive state championships.

He moved to Aspen after convincing his petite wife, Louise, she could win the grueling 22-mile Leadville Pack Burro Race over some of the roughest terrain the Colorado Rockies could muster. She did and won $1,000, a sufficient grubstake for the Kuhns to resettle in Aspen. Heiko was a naturally gifted athlete. Shortly after arriving he became a golf professional and was chosen the first pro at the new Snowmass Golf Course. He was fun to play with and we often teamed up to play together. He was very competitive and wanted — no, had — to win whatever the game or contest.

Around the Western Slope of Colorado there was a pro-am tournament at one of the region's courses at least once a month. Heiko was anxious to put a good team together from the Aspen-Snowmass area to compete in these regional contests. He needed a low, middle and high handicapper to round out his team. He chose me as his low, the mayor of Snowmass as his middle player, and one of a myriad of congenial, mediocre golfers to round out the team.

I was in my mid-30s age-wise and was a decent striker of the ball from tee to green, but occasionally I got a case of the putting "Yips." The "Yips" are an involuntary jerking in the lower arm and hand muscles while making an easy putting stroke. It is so frustrating and hard to overcome that it has caused major PGA golf champions to cry and quit the game. To help me with this problem I was using a very heavy putter that was made out of a big chunk of white marble. I took a lot of ribbing because of the way it looked. It was huge, heavy and butt-ugly but I thought it was effective.

Because occasional "Yips" caused me to miss easy putts, Heiko probably would have replaced me as his number-one player, but I was also a pilot and owned a Cessna 210 that could carry six passengers or a team of four husky pro-am golfers with their heavy clubs. Naturally, my position on the team as player/pilot was set in stone, and we flew to most of the tournaments.

One tournament was in Craig, Colorado, a remote coal mining and ranching community up near the Wyoming border. The course was typical of those in small western Colorado towns: nine holes probably laid out some years ago by a bored farmer with a plow, disc, harrow and some leftover grass seed. Usually there was some water in crisscrossing irrigation ditches and lots of stately cottonwoods over-hanging the narrow fairways. The greens were always small and not the smoothest. Craig's nine holes fit the mold perfectly.

Our team was competitive and honest, but several other teams had sandbaggers, players with manufactured high handicaps who could shoot lights out when they wanted to. On this particular Friday our team was tied with another team who were notorious sandbagging cheaters. On the 18th hole I had an easy 19-inch tap-in putt to win and put those crummy cheating bastards away. Plus, if we won, everyone on our team got $250 of the prize money

I thought, "Steady now, this is an easy putt for all the marbles. Back and through, back and through. Smooth it now — smooooth!" YIP! It squirted by the hole and never touched it, and we lost!

Dejected the whole team loaded into the Cessna for the long ride back to Sardy Field in Aspen. Somewhere over Mount Sopris, at 14,000-feet, the Cessna's side window suddenly blew open and a gi-ant rush of air bombarded the cockpit. Shocked, I screamed over the deafening noise, "CLOSE THAT WINDOW!" They did and the quiet returned. Over the engine hum I heard a muted snicker and when I glanced into the back seat everyone guffawed loudly.

Heiko had thrown my putter out the window.

I didn't miss my marble putter very long. Heiko sold me, at his cost, a Ping putter out of his shop, and with that Ping I happily got rid of the "Yips."

Every time Heiko and I got together we laughed about the possibility that some rancher sitting on his horse saw that putter fly from the sky and bury itself in the ground, and the startled cowboy looked up into the heavens and said,

"Damn! God must have missed his putt!"

CHAPTER 38

What's a Microwave?

MICROWAVE 101

Streaking along at warp speed we 70 or 80-somethings are swept up in a frantic ever-changing techno-world. It is hard to fathom how different our life is today from the snail's pace of a few decades ago. Not many years ago we were setting little pieces of lead type by hand in order to print a page. Then came the typewriter with carbon sheets if you wanted copies. Remember the smell of the mimeographed pages? Our grandchildren have no idea what a typewriter or a mimeograph machine is, or how technically difficult our life was way back when.

I just read that it will not be a meager one hundred years of techno advancement in the twenty-first century. According to the article, technology is growing at an exponential rate, and we can expect two thousand years of advancement in the next ninety years. Huh?

The first tech message was sent in 1992, and now there are over 31 billion Google requests every month. Since most of us old guys left a lot of our brains on the third stool at the Jerome Bar, how can any of us codgers wrap what's left of our brains around something going so fast? We can't! We can't even fake it. My 10-year-old grandson, Jack, has to program the DVD player for me every time I want to use it.

This techno-crap may leave us old farts behind but it doesn't reduce our curiosity about it, especially when some new confusing contraption comes on the scene — like the microwave oven did many years ago.

Good friends Bette and John Oakes threw a surprise birthday bash for Marsha (More on that party later). That was in the mid '70s and Bette and John had just remodeled their kitchen. At that party John was anxious to show all of their guests the new technological advances they'd installed, such as their new microwave oven.

While the ladies gabbed away in the dining room, John assembled the men in the kitchen to demonstrate his remarkable new gadget. In a blink of an eye, he proudly boiled some water and then cooked some sizzling bacon. We were in awe and dutifully impressed but then he mentioned that no metal could be placed in a microwave oven nor could you zap eggs.

"What, no eggs? Come on, man! What could happen to a tiny little egg?"

With our prodding, John agreed to a test. We put four un-cracked eggs in a shallow plate in the microwave oven, closed the door and set the timer on high. We, of great faith, gathered around the small oven window to watch the eggs do whatever they weren't supposed to do.

A couple of minutes passed and we Einsteins smugly shrugged our shoulders and — **Kaboom!**

What happened was a miracle, a miracle that no one was hurt, a miracle that the Oakes were able to find all the tiny fragments of those little bombs. We might as well have put a couple of dynamite sticks in the microwave as those nasty eggs violently blew the oven door open, and millions of BB-sized shards of hot eggshells, yolks and whites blew all over us curious, but stupid, observers and every cabinet, window, sink, floor and ceiling within 10 yards of the blast.

Before the Oakes could ask for help in cleaning up the disaster scene, the defeated kitchen techno-warriors took inventory of body parts, grabbed their astonished wives and beat a hasty retreat. "Ah, ... er ... goodnight, Bette. Goodnight, John. Loved the evening, love your new kitchen. Have to run — young babysitter, you know. Ta ta!"

CHAPTER 39

Pay Me Child Support ... or Else

I've established that my wife, Marsha, is also a joker. The story I'm going to tell didn't happen in Aspen but we were living there at the time so it counts.

This is a good one she pulled on a high school friend at my twentieth class reunion in 1971. I had graduated from East High School in Denver. It was a large three-year, sophomore through senior, school with more than 2,600 students. Our class was 685 big. Even after three years, it was impossible to know each of them beyond a passing "Hi" in the hallways.

Reunions have a life of their own. At the tenth, everyone's 28 and if they don't have a professional career as a doctor, CPA or a lawyer, they'll reluctantly tell you what they are doing but quickly follow it up with who they're going to be. It's all expectations. Inquiring, you'll hear:

"Well, right now I'm delivering milk but I just put a down payment on a commercial property and I'm going to build an 82-unit high-rise apartment. We're just waiting on financing before we break ground."

"I'm a lifeguard now but I've been offered four positions as a stockbroker with all the big Wall Street houses. I just can't decide which firm I like the best."

"I'm clerking in my father-in-law's hardware store, but Suzie and I are going to move to Napa Valley and buy a boutique winery."

Ten years later reality sets in and the same but now 38-year-old alums say:

"I really like my job with Meadow Gold. They have a fabulous retirement plan."

"Being a Lifeguard really is good for the body. See what great shape I'm in. I'm tan and I meet a lot of young chicks."

"Come by the hardware tomorrow, we've got a great sale on hand tools."

Alas, ten years later at the thirtieth, we are now 48 and we all admit, "Man, I can't wait for Social Security and retirement. I can't stand this rat race anymore."

At any reunion the spouses feel out of place unless they've had a lot of previous contact with other spouses.

My classmate and cousin Jim Colfer and his wife, Gwen, double-dated with Marsha and me to our twentieth East High reunion. We were beyond fashionably late and everyone was already sitting down to dinner. We couldn't find any two chairs together and were forced to split up. We were all at the same long banquet table that sat about 30. Marsha was at one end and I was at the other. If I wanted to communicate with her I'd have to use sign language. That was OK — we'd get by.

Sitting directly across from Marsha was Ron Epstein. Ron was tall with curly red hair, and had a catawampus smile that was often mistaken for a smart-alecky sneer. His intelligence made his wit both scathing and quick, a trait he inherited from his devious father. Ron's father was touted as one of the best defense lawyers in Denver and maybe that is why he was so conniving, but it was disastrous for his son. He could disguise his voice so it sounded just like Ron's. As a habit he answered the home phone in his son's voice. He also could recognize the voices of Ron's friends.

Ring Ring. "Hello"

"Hey, Ron, it's ... "

"Hi, Jack!"

"Hey, do you think you can get your old man's car tonight? A whole bunch of us are going out to Daniel's Park for a kegger. Jerry's brother bought the beer for us and everyone's going. And that hot big-boobed chick Carmen you got a crush on will be there — it will be a blast!"

Long pause

"Hello?"

"Just a minute, Jack. I'll go get Ron."

"Oh, shit!"

Longer pause

Ron screamed into the phone, "Brendlinger, what the hell did you say to my old man? I'm grounded for two weeks!" Click.

You know at reunions everyone has a nametag. If they didn't it would be a bunch of bewildered alums walking around like zombies muttering, "Do I know you?" "Do you know me?"

Name-tagged Marsha was sitting across from Ron, and he noticed Marsha Brendlinger was written on her badge. Despite my faux pas with his father, Ron and I were pretty close in school, and he pleasantly said across the table, "You must be Jack's wife?"

I don't know what got into her, as we'd been married eleven years, but she coyly answered, "Yes, yes I am. In fact, we're newlyweds."

Ron at first didn't know whether to believe her but didn't want to offend her, so he said, "Oh, how long have you been married?"

She batted her lashes and softly murmured, "Three days."

My cousin Jim was just a few seats away and overheard the conversation. Ron knew Jim and I had stayed close and he turned to Jim and said, "This lady across from me says she just got married to Brendlinger! I don't believe it."

Jim, a superb salesman in the world of high finance, was always quick on his feet, "Oh yeah, Gwen and I stood up for them just a few days ago in Las Vegas."

Still skeptical but wavering, Ron turned to Marsha and said, "Are you his first wife?"

Batting her eyes again, Marsha answered, "Oh, no, he was married for ten years before I met him. He left her and his kids for me."

Ron was getting more and more confused. "Who…who was he married to before?"

Jim heard this and interjected with a name of a girlfriend I had dated in the ninth and tenth grades. "Jack was married to Donna Lou Mendenhall and they have two kids, both girls," Jim announced.

Ron was now completely dumbfounded because in the cobwebs of his memory he thought Donna Lou had married a guy named Moore and he said so, albeit tentatively.

Before she started to giggle, Marsha excused herself and went to the ladies room. At the mirror, doctoring her makeup, who should be doing the same but Donna Lou Mendenhall Moore. Marsha introduced herself, explained the joke to Donna Lou and asked if she wanted to play along. Always game for fun, Donna Lou enthusiastically agreed and told Marsha to go back to the table and she would follow.

Marsha was not sure what Donna Lou had up her sleeve. She marched up behind Marsha and, in a sneering whisper but loud enough for Ron to hear, she growled, "Home-wrecker!" Then she stomped along the table to where I sat, minding my own business and completely unaware of the joke, slapped me in the back of the head and yelled loud enough for the whole table of 30 to hear, "You cheapskate, you're two months behind in child support payments. Pay up or I'll have your butt back in front of the judge!" and stomped off.

Marsha and Jim were roaring, Ron's face was in his soup and I was standing agape, jerking my head back and forth and pleading innocent —the only time in my life I was.

CHAPTER 40

Sock It To Me! Sock It To Me!

At the same twentieth reunion Marsha played her "newlywed" prank, another practical joke was being staged by a classmate that is worth a chapter.

At a twentieth reunion, everyone, especially the 38-year-old men, think they are still 20. The body is a couple of inches from where it used to be, there is a recognizable and ebbing hairline, and most of their thinking is still two-and-a-half feet below the brain. This is the perfect scenario for this prank.

A two-lane parkway with a mowed grass strip between the lanes ran in front of East High. In the warm sun of fall and spring this strip of lawn was a favorite picnic spot for the students to sit and eat their sack lunches, enjoy the rays and eyeball each other. It was also ideal for the longhaired, white T-shirted, cigarettes rolled up in their sleeves, toothpicks just showing in the corner of their mouths hot-rodders to drag up and down the parkway, showing off their chopped, lowered, de-chromed and candy-appled creations.

After World War II, families were still struggling just to get back to even, and there wasn't any money to buy cars for the parents, let alone kids in high school. Transportation was school bus, streetcar, bike (nobody cool rode bikes because they were all fat-tired clunkers and you had to wear a pant-leg clip, which wasn't cool.) Most students just footed it everywhere in our penny loafers. If a student had a car, he was popular — very popular. However, the hotrod boys weren't as popular as their car-owning status would imply. Oh yeah, they appealed to the girls who wore black knee-length skirts so tight that they could hardly walk and they had to take short little ridiculous steps, one shoe in front of the other. It looked as if something was stuck up there where things shouldn't be stuck. They wore their hair up in a ponytail but, instead of a rubber band, they wrapped it with a bright folded-up scarf. The rodders were notoriously poor students because they usually worked at a gas station or garage so their entire life was wrapped up in their hotrod. Auto Mechanics was their only "A."

One of these guys I'll call "Mick". Mick loved his car and was only squeaking by in school. If the yearbook chose the student most likely NOT to succeed, Mick would have been the frontrunner. Since graduation 20 years ago, no one had seen or heard from him — until the reunion.

At the reunion, Mick waited until most of the alums and their spouses had seated themselves at the long banquet tables surrounding the dance floor before he made his entrance. Oh, and what an entrance it was! He was elegantly decked out in a blazing white, very expensive linen suit with a black silky shirt and a white linen tie. A white panama straw fedora, jauntily cocked, topped it off. Mick's apparel was a showstopper but unexceptional compared to what was on his arm: a woman —and I mean woman. She was incredible! Long, slightly curled, blond tresses swayed in time with her swinging hips. Hips and the rest of her were crammed into a gold lamé, backless sheath cocktail dress that was not off some May Company or Penny's rack. Over one shoulder and cascading down her bare tan back was a white mink stole that would set back Aga Kahn's gold stash. She was alarmingly statuesque and classy beautiful — everything in the right places, well, maybe a bit top heavy, but I didn't notice. Remember, Marilyn Monroe hadn't been discovered yet so all the men were thinking, "Yeah, a blond Jane Russell."

Every eye was glued to Mick and his Jane; the only thing missing from this grand entry was the band playing "Hail to the Chief."

Mick had obviously bribed one of the catering waiters because a nice table for two suddenly appeared just to the left and in the warm glow of the bandstand spotlights.

They had the total attention of the gawkers…the wives slightly shaking their heads and tsk-tsking and their husbands, mouths agape, were staring with stupid, cheshire cat, slightly slobbering grins. The hall was surprisingly quiet except for a thud when some perturbed wife slugged her husband on the upper arm. The dinner went on normally except for an occasional glance in Mick and Jane's direction. They seemed content, very amorous and sexually attentive to each other.

Following dinner there were the usual droning speeches and toasts to the alma mater and then the band fired up the dance music. No rock 'n' roll for this aging group — everything was a big-band jitterbug or a dreamy slow number. After a few numbers, Mick and Jane got up to a slow ballad. Jane, seemingly giggly and tipsy, was dancing close, noticeably close. Mick turned halfway through the number and tapped one of the other couples and suggested they switch dancing partners. All the males wished silently, "That lucky stiff, why wasn't that me?"

With every enviable male eye on the lucky guy, Jane snuggled her beautiful head into his shoulder, reared back her hips and —KACHINK — stuck it to him, grinding, grinding. Suddenly every male, including the bandleader, the chef, seven waiters and a dishwasher were trying to cut in or get on her dance card. All through the night it was KACHING, GRIND, KABOOM, GRIND, KACHING, GRIND. Mick sat at his table all alone, peacock proud, smoking a long, thin Havana cheroot.

Peeved wives had had enough and unsatisfied husbands were reluctantly on their way home and getting a well-deserved earful and nothing else for the rest of the night.

The jokester Mick, the yearbook's ne'er-do-well frontrunner and now an owner of a successful Albuquerque auto dealership, happily gathered up his Jane, left the empty dancehall and took her back to her regular job as Miss Roxanne Ryder, the number-one erotic dancer for Sid King's titty bar on Colfax Avenue.

KACHING!

CHAPTER 41

Streaking

Even though I didn't know them well at the time, I loved the story I heard Aspen natives Don Stapleton (Stape) and Tony Vagnuer and their girlfriends played on the hippies in town. During their heavy smoking and drinking days these two natives were my kind of crazy.

It was in the late 1960s and it was hippy time in both Aspen and the rest of the country. In that era of free love and tie-dyed shirts, streaking was a craze in public places. Streakers, male or female, in the nude, were seen running across the field at almost any major football or baseball game. Things-a-flopping, they were outsprinting fat ushers and pudgy security men. The crowds loved it.

One warm summer day in Owl Creek at the Stapleton's homestead log cabin, Stape, Tony and their girlfriends were well into their second bottle of scotch, and the whiskey-fueled partiers began an impromptu game of grab-ass. The giggling and horsing around led to a torn shirt, then a yanked-off blouse sleeve, and next all were naked and laughing hysterically.

Stape's girlfriend said, "Hey, you drunks, all this bare skin shouldn't go to waste. Let's jump in my VW bug and cruise around town — free as the jaybirds of nakedness fame." And they did.

In those days there was no down-valley bus service, so the town had erected two Thumbing Stations for the convenience of hitchhikers. One station was on Main Street in front of the motel, the Aspen Court, and the other was in front of the Forest Service Office next to the S-curves.

Driving by, the buffed-down drunks saw a hippie thumbing for a ride and they said, "Mmmm, I wonder what he'd do if we offered him a ride?" They screeched up to the curb, rolled down the window and yelled, "Hey, bro, we're headed to Basalt. Do you want a ride?" "You bet!" answered the unsuspecting hiker.

The car doors flew open to reveal four lily-white unclad bodies beckoning him. Mouth agape, eyes as wide as a competition Frisbee, the hippie stammered, "Uh … er … um, no thanks! They tried again and again but no takers. They were amazed at the shocked response from several hippies both male and female. "Hell," snickered Stape, a Viet Nam vet. "I'm really disappointed, I thought all these friggin hippies were into free love and naked freedoms."

Although they had thoughtfully brought along their cigarettes, they had no matches because they had no pockets. They were driving on Cooper Street (before there was a pedestrian mall) and approaching the Red Onion on the right. Tony said he knew there was always a cup full of wooden matches on the end of the Onion bar, so he challenged the girls to dash into the bar, get a fistful of matches and dash back to the bug. Don's girl said, "Ah, what the hell, I'll do it!" She streaked into the bar, grabbed a handful of matches, and set a 40-yard-dash record back to the car as there were several old miners hobbling after her. "Hey, li'l missy, come on back! Let me buy ya a beer."

The moral of that story is: If you're naked, hippies are OK, but stay away from any old miners.

Streaking II

Another, unrelated, streaking incident in Aspen happened on the last day of a ski season during that late '60s hallucinogenic period. It was a ritual to celebrate the closing day with an enormous party at Merry-Go-Round restaurant, midway up Aspen Highlands. The tourists were long gone to Chicago, Atlanta and Tuscaloosa, and it was time for local skiers to chill out and have some fun.

The restaurant has a big deck facing the mountain that catches the sun and views of skiers taking the bumps on Gunbarrel run. The deck was jam-packed with revelers and the beer was pouring like Niagara. Everyone had a perfect view (for some it was fuzzy) of the upper half of the mountain. It was a beautiful, very warm April day and everyone was in short sleeves and bikini tops and the snow was turning softer and slushier under the hot sun.

Two couples, probably tanked, stoned — or both, decided it would be a perfect time to go up the lift, ski down to a big concealing blue spruce, strip off their ski duds, and then schuss in a streak by the thousands of partiers on the deck. They'd be going so fast no one would recognize them. Perfect!

Butt-naked, all four burst from behind the tree, hooping and hollering to attract attention and, as planned, they were skiing so fast they were unrecognizable.

Aha, but jokester Mother Nature stepped in and on the flats, right in front of the crowded deck, the snow had become deep sticky cement, and the four speeding streakers were no longer streaking but ground to an embarrassing (good choice of word here) stop right in front of the thousands of screaming, pointing and guffawing crowd. In what seemed forever, the hapless, butt-naked foursome was forced to painstakingly plod through the sloppy slush some 50 yards before they were beyond the building and headed downhill again.

It was doubly embarrassing for the red-faced male nudes because it wasn't that warm!

Streaking III

This one is similar to the story of Stape, Tony and their girlfriends streaking the Red Onion, but it has a delightful practical-joke twist. Two couples (whose names will go unmentioned to protect the guilty) were partying and enjoying the unusually warm afternoon of a glorious Aspen summer day in the mid 1960s. Cruising around town, more than a bit bored and on the backside of tipsy, the boys dared the girls to streak naked across Aspen's Main Street in front of Matthew's Drug. With an air of liquor bravado, the girls took the dare.

The plan was for the men to pull the car up to the crosswalk, the girls would jump out in the altogether, hightail it across the street and the driver would pull a U-turn and they would jump in — slick as a bare-assed whistle. One, two, three — Go! The girls jumped out in their birthday suits, hand-in-hand and shrieking streaked across the four lanes. When they turned to jump back in the waiting car, the boys, still on the other side of the street, honked, waved, smiled and DROVE OFF!

CHAPTER 42

When I say Jump, You Jump!

Why is it I seem to surround myself with witty, sarcastic, funny people? Maybe I'm covering up for my closetful of inadequacies.

Witty, sarcastic, sharp as a stropped razor, quick as a hummingbird's wings, hysterically funny Howard Englander came into my life in the mid 1960s. He and his first wife, Marion, moved to Aspen from Chicago because he was interested in buying half of the only fm radio station in the region, KSNO. When he first arrived he was the station's morning personality and disc Jockey. Oh my gosh, he was funny! I think it was the first time I'd ever listened to the radio in between songs. Howard's humor was subtle; it didn't up and hit you between the ears. You had to think while you were listening or you'd miss half the numerous, humorous innuendos. I knew immediately we were going to be friends and went on a quest to meet him. I was right, our times in each other's company was a back-and-forth tennis match, a volley of giggly zingers. Point, set, match went to Howard as I wasn't able to return all the sarcastic smashes. I think Cossel and Rickles, both masters of the barb, would have been ball boys in a match with Howard.

The KSNO buy didn't work out and marketing smart Howard was hired as advertising director for the new ski resort of Snowmass Village. At the same time, Howard, Marion (Howard's wife), Marsha and I decided to open a fondue restaurant in the Clock Tower building in Snowmass Village. After hours of deliberation and creative brainstorming we named it...The Tower Fondue Restaurant. I was to design and build the restaurant structure and Howard and Marion were to operate it. It was really a neat eatery concept with do-it-yourself fondue everything, the standard cheese and bread, plus filets of beef seared in oil, Swiss raclette and hot fudge fondue over every fruit or cake imaginable.

Our concept was great but none of the new restaurants in Snowmass did well that first season because everyone continued to go into Aspen for the famous eateries like the Jerome, Golden Horn, Red Onion and the Copper Kettle. We soon realized that our restaurant wasn't going to keep two families going so we instigated our buy-sell agreement and Howard bought our half. A year later he sold it to John Denver, who dropped the fondue and successfully operated it for many years as a family restaurant that featured entertaining bartenders and waiters who were tableside magicians.

To say the least, Howard was not an accomplished skier when he arrived in Aspen. He was game, however, to the point that he was a menace to himself and anyone within a mountain or two. Since our honeymoon Marsha's skiing had improved 100-fold. (In fact, now at age 75, ski instructors, who don't even know her, stop her on the hill and tell her she makes a perfect turn. I've skied hard for 69 years and

her recognition and "perfect turn" should piss me off, but it doesn't —
I'm wildly proud of her.

Back in 1966, however, her perfect skiing was still in the Parallel
Ski Turn 101 stage, and Howard was looking for a ski companion who
wouldn't make fun and laugh at his non-breathing, tippy-toeing, re-
verse-shouldered, hip-rotating, double-pole planting, semi-stepped
stem Christie. Why he thought Marsha would laugh, I'm not sure as
he was an absolute master of that technique. Howard also knew that
Marsha, a compassionate Florence Nightingale in Bogners, would
not leave him stranded and would stay with him until the ambulance
arrived.

They had fun skiing together and were always bantering about
who was the better of the two. To any knowledgeable eye, Marsha
was clearly superior, but Howard had that I-can-do-it attitude and
he wasn't about to give in. They kept finding small challenges on the
slopes and, in their best imitation of Betty Hutton and Howard Keel,
they'd belt out, "I can ski anything faster than you can!" "No, you can't!
I can ski anything faster than you." " No, you can't! "Yes, I can!" "No!"
"Yes!" And off they'd go, neither skiing it fast nor well because they
were out-of-control laughing.

One warm spring day they were bombing the bunny hill at
Buttermilk and Howard said giggling, "I can ski-jump farther than you
can!" "No, you can't! I can jump farther than you!" "No, you can't!"
"Yes, I can!"

Unfortunately for the two of them, their bravado banter was overheard by Rollie Herberg, the CEO of the Janss Corporation's development team for the village at the base of Snowmass. Rollie was a superb
and knowledgeable construction executive who built the enormous
base village in a blink of an eye. As an astute, revered CEO, you'd think
he'd always be serious but that was a calculated front. He could put on
his other hat and be as funny and mischievous as the rest of us — and
the rest of us were never serious.

"Ahaa!" Rollie said to the startled Marsha and Howard. "We are going to have a big jump event starring you two sorry braggers. On the last day of the season you two will perform a ski jump and the one who loses will have to wear a plaster cast on their leg for a month," he proclaimed.

Agape and gasping, their bluff called, Marsha said to Howard. "You'll chicken out quicker than I do!" "No, I won't chicken out quicker than you do!" "Yes, you will!" "No, I won't!" "Will!" "Won't!" The stage was set. The contest was on.

Rollie made a big deal of it, and he ran a couple of ads in the Aspen Times:

Hear Ye! Hear Ye!
Come One! Come All to the Ski Jump
Contest of the Year.
A Daring Contest of Flying On Skis
Featuring: Marsha"Flying Walenda" Brendlinger
Versus
Howard "Evel Knievel" Englander
Buttermilk Bunny Hill

11am Sunday, April 3rd

Now neither Marsha nor Howard had ever jumped anything except the chalk lines in schoolyard hopscotch and both had a miserable week awaiting their unknown fate. The day arrived and there actually was an interested small crowd of bloodthirsty spectators hoping for the worst or, at least, a giggle or two.

Ski jumps are measured by the distance a jumper is expected to travel in the air. Therefore, a 60-meter jump has an expected jumping flight of 196 feet. A 90-meter Olympic jump estimates the distance of flight would be about the length of a football field. To make the contest between Marsha and Howard exciting, I shoveled up a bunch of snow and prepared a jump 30.48 centimeters high with a rating of 2 meters so the frightened contestants would be soaring a scary 6.4 feet.

Some 45 feet above the takeoff, both contestants were visibly shaken. They played scissors, paper and stone to see who was first and Howard lost. Howard pointed his skis toward the jump and lowered his head between his poles. He held that stationary position a long time. He obviously was praying. He's Jewish, but he wasn't taking any chances and I swear I saw him make the sign of the cross. Fear etched in his face, barely moving and arms wind-milling, he flopped off the takeoff for a distance of 6.5 feet and a quarter inch. He was bellowing his approval as he raised his arms in triumph and snowplowed to a stop. Marsha at the top nodded to the challenge. A good staunch Mormon, she knew if she died she would still attain a high level in heaven so she pushed off confidently. Man, look at her go! Skiing twice as fast as Howard, Marsha actually tried to jump off the takeoff. She soared so far past Howard's distance, we put the tape measures back in our parkas. Victorious? No! Marsha was careless in the outrun, caught an edge, fell and slid up to a smirking, fist-pumping Howard.

The rules stated that you had to stand up clear through the outrun. She'd lost. Afterwards, on the deck behind the Buttermilk restaurant and surrounded by spectators, beer, wine and laughter, Rollie stood on a picnic table and read a proclamation he had prepared and written on a Roman-like scroll. It was long and hysterically funny with lots of whom it may concerns, wherebys and whereases.

The rules also stated that the loser had to wear a plaster cast on their leg for a month. Rollie and I took Marsha down to the office of Dr. Bugsy Barnard, who had worked on more bones than a Brontosaurus Rex paleontologist at the Smithsonian. Bugsy said he wouldn't dare put a cast on a leg that wasn't broken. "What would that do to my reputation?"

Rollie pulled out a C note and Bugsy grabbed the plaster gauze. "Oh, hell," he said, "My reputation's not worth a shit anyway!"

CHAPTER 43

He Did What In My Toilet?

While we are in the vicinity of Howard Englander and Rollie Herberg I best tell a story of when they were neighbors in a duplex in East Aspen. As you read in the previous story these two gentlemen were new arrivals to Aspen but already pillars of the community. But that didn't keep them from having a tongue-in-cheek air of mischievousness about them.

The duplex they were renting had a small vestibule in front of each of their front doors and Howard, having heard of my plowing in Peter Greene's front door, took that cue and one snowy night he crept over to Rollie's vestibule and shoveled it full of snow and ice. He expected an immediate response from Rollie but none came. Rollie, who was the CEO of the construction of the new Snowmass village, merely had one of his laborers come and de-shovel it. Nary a word to the hapless Howard.

But, Howard knew there was probably a "Get Even" in his future and with trepidation he waited and waited, constantly looking over his shoulder for the inevitable.

Rollie waited until he knew Howard was having a dinner party with important town folk. Then, before the party, when Howard and his wife were out buying preparations for the party Rollie snuck in and packed, and I mean packed, both of Howard's toilets with snow and ice. As a coup de grace he then poured a bucket of water with a yellow food dye over the ice and snow.

Totally shocked, and minutes before his guests were to arrive, finicky Howard was forced to chip out the yellow mess with rubber gloves and a clothes pin over his nose.

CHAPTER 44

Don't Leave Home Without 'Em!

Before I tell a few stories about her, I need to give you some insight to Marsha, my wife. She is a remarkable, caring, loving, down-to-earth woman who wants to mother the world (every acquaintance reading this is nodding their head in agreement).

Every morning, yes, every morning for the last 30 of our 54 years together she gets up at the crack of dawn to bake six or seven dozen chocolate-chip cookies and a couple of banana breads with a caramel walnut frosting. Not for me, mind you, I'm already too fat, but for anyone in her realm that may need a treat. If you have a hangnail, call her and your sweet tooth is covered for a month. She's famous for her cookies. Even if he doesn't have a delivery, our UPS driver comes to the house to get his free cookie fix.

I made her some thank-you cards on my computer that she's too embarrassed to use. On the front of the card there is a NASA picture of the Earth from outer space, and the caption says, "Marsha's Sphere of Friends." Believe me, it is not much of an exaggeration. It takes her two hours to buy a quart of milk as she knows everyone in the store and she has to talk to them all.

She is a teacher by degree, but for a career she's a homemaker, baker, cook, bottle washer, mother, spouse, nursemaid, choreographer, marathoner, fundraiser, board member, psychiatrist, and most of all a damn good tireless friend to everyone, whether she knows them or not.

In the fifty-four years we've been married, I've called her "Velcro," as every wayward soul looking for a couple of delicious squares and a clean pillow to lay his or her head sticks to her like epoxy glue to a broken toy. She's like the little, wide-eyed kid who comes home dragging a dirty, smelly puppy saying, "Daddy look what followed me home! Can I keep him? Huh? Can I? Huh?" The list of lost kids, homeless families, foreign students, hungry hobos, wayward expatriates, estranged spouses and gifted athletes who have found refuge within our walls would fill the pages of an urban phonebook. Everyone rightfully calls her Ma B. Nobody calls me Pa B. — I'm mostly ignored. I just get to pay for it all.

Nothing about her should perturb me, but something does: She is a damn know-it-all. If anyone in the valley wants to know anything, from how to prepare something in the kitchen to what to do with their wild teenager, Marsha has the answer.

I was dating her when the Peanuts cartoon first appeared. Charlie Brown's nemesis, Lucy, was Marsha incarnate, a cute dark-haired, round-faced, big-mouthed, gleam-in-her-eye, know-it-all. Besides giving Charlie Brown a bad time, one of Lucy's traits was that she considered herself a psychiatrist. She stood in front of a homemade cardboard booth with a hand-printed sign saying "Psychiatry 5 Cents." That's my Marsha. People, even strangers, call her all the time for advice. She stays on the phone with them for hours and, dang it, she doesn't even charge them 5 cents.

People also call her for the local gossip. She says she's not a gossip because everything she knows is fact, and, according to her, facts are not gossip. So Marsha just spreads facts. Some of them are juicy, tell-all facts but, nonetheless, they are facts, not gossip.

When our children, Kurt, Eric, Dina and Kira, were growing up, they couldn't get away with anything as their mother's sphere of influence went way beyond their small circle. She knew all about the my-parents-aren't-home parties long before they did. They were frustrated but knowing that their mother probably already knew everything kept them pretty good kids.

As knowledgeable as she is, Marsha can also be naïve in a childlike way. Her mother Helen was that way too. One spring our family was visiting the grandparents, Max and Helen, on the California peninsula south of San Francisco. I think we were driving around looking for a bowling alley when Helen saw a sign, GRAN PRIX, on a large building that housed tracks for those miniature slot-racing cars. Helen, innocently and without thinking, blurted, "Grand Pricks! Oh my, Max, they must have some big ones in there!"

The following story highlights Marsha's naiveté. Our lodge, The Applejack Inn, was a member of the nationwide chain, Best Western. We belonged because they were recognized as a superior lodging organization and they were an excellent source of reservations in the summer and off-seasons. However, they were a pain in the neck when we didn't need to fill rooms in the winter.

Best Western held its annual convention in Las Vegas every September and each member was required to attend. We hated the convention and never went to the meetings but didn't mind going because we loved Vegas — not for the gambling, mind you, but for all the recreational opportunities that abound in the Vegas area that no one in those days used or even knew about. We crammed our days with golf, tennis, swimming, water-skiing, hiking, spa visits, biking and lounging. At night we would dress up and catch a show.

We usually flew down to Vegas in my plane with an off-the-wall, hip couple, Judy and Don Sabin. Don was in Aspen real estate and Judy was a perennial debutante. They were children of the '60s and didn't want to miss any joys, pharmaceutical or otherwise. Marsha and I tolerated their excesses because they were just plain fun. Shortly after we arrived in Vegas, Judy and Marsha went shopping and agreed to live it up a little by purchasing beautiful sheer, see-through blouses for our dress-up night. Both ladies had attractive chests that most would die for, but conservative Marsha was concerned and bought a same-color bra as a backup. Judy was disappointed so she convinced Marsha to also buy those half-cup, stick-on thingamajigs that gave support and some, but not total, coverage. Marsha's concern was although the nightclubs were in subdued light, the casinos were not. That evening, at Judy's and my insistence, Marsha elected not to wear the backup bra and she put on the sticky half-cups. They worked, and Don and I thought both ladies looked bouncily beautifully fashionable and sexy.

We had a ball and stayed out until after 3 a.m. I quickly jumped into bed anxiously awaiting my risqué roommate. I waited and waited and then heard a long, tortuous groan from the bathroom and hurried to see what was wrong. I had to bite my lip. Marsha was crouched naked on the toilet, grotesquely bent over the sink with one boob in the sink under hot water. The sticky half-bras were stuck solid to her skin and wouldn't budge. Neither the hot water nor anything she did loosened their painful adhesiveness.

For two hours we peeled the sticky globs bit-by-bit and piece-by-piece from her shredded orbs. Even in the Vegas' heat Marsha went bra-less for several painful days and wore a ski parka and a sweater over a soft turtleneck. Her risqué days were over, or so I thought.

A couple of years later on the celebration of our anniversary, she longingly looked at that beautiful see-through blouse and matching bra and asked me if I thought she should wear it for our romantic dinner at one of Aspen's darker restaurants. It is not wise to play a practical joke on your wife as they have too many disastrous, unspeakable ways to get even. But sometimes a joker has to do what he has to do and I said, "Hon, that is a beautiful and expensive blouse and it doesn't look right with that cumbersome bra. Why don't you go without it? It's very dark in Stromberg's anyway." She agreed, but over 'em she put on one of my mothers hand-me-down furs to keep 'em hidden and warm.

What I didn't tell her was that we were not going to Stromberg's for dinner because our friends were throwing us a surprise dinner party at John and Bette Oakes' house.

I told her that we were stopping by the Oakes' as they had a gift for us and told her we would be there only a minute or two so she wouldn't have to take her coat off. Then — SURPRISE! HAPPY ANNIVERSARY, MARSHA AND JACK

OH OH! She knew I was in on this party and the look on her face was not one of surprise but a nasty, dirty one, throwing darts my way. She knew she couldn't endure a sit-down dinner swathed in a fur coat so she grinned and bared it. She was absolutely adorable, but miserable in her athletic, yoga gyrations trying to keep 'em covered. I'm sure every one of the partiers thought she was in the first stages of cerebral palsy. But I loved her because every now and then she deliberately flashed me a quick photo-op view that made me want to take her home early.

Now that we're in our 70s, if she wants me to see 'em through her clothing she'll have to wear a see-through skirt.

CHAPTER 45
Chugalug 101

HEE HEE HEE!

In college I took a class that carried over into my "mature" years that sometimes paid off in Aspen's many bars and nightclubs. It was my most interesting and successful class and I took from "Professor" Charlie Butcher in Suite One A in the basement of the Kappa Sig house: How to drink beer by just pouring it down your throat without swallowing, or Chugalug 101. It was one of the few classes I ever got an A plus. After 30 or 40 demonstration beers, Charlie would have given axe-wielding, keg-busting temperance leader Carrie Nation an A.

It was one of the most expensive classes I ever took because, as tuition, I had to pay for the beer. After months and months of hard training, (someone had to do it!) I was challenging the hand quickness and guzzling speed of my mentor, and it only took me a micro-second to lift a full beer and slap down an empty glass. I was usually fast enough that my unsuspecting opponent hadn't even gotten his glass to his lips. Throughout my college career my class excellence paid for many a night of free drinking and, to boot, some hard cash in the pocket.

During my "you ought to know better" 30's in Aspen I could occasionally be persuaded to a demonstration (if there was a bet, you know!). One night a good number of us were enjoying a nightcap or two at the nightclub below the Golden Horn restaurant. Howard Englander, witty radio DJ and the first advertising director for Snowmass ski resort, bet me twenty dollars that he could chug a beer faster than I could drink two. Recently I had beaten him with a full glass to his empty one and realized how slow his hand speed was, so I gratefully accepted.

"Five, four, three, two, one, GO!" Chug, chug and my two glasses were down. I glanced up to see everyone at the table laughing and pointing at sheepish Howard while a screaming person was gasping behind him. His practical joke all along was simply to throw the beer out of his glass over his shoulder. Little did he know that our ever-attentive waitress, in her revealing off-shoulder dirndl, was standing right behind Howard. Not only did I win twenty dollars but laughingly watched hapless Howard lay a big tip on the startled, irate and beer-soaked waitress.

CHAPTER 46
Fifty Years of Fun and Games

Here it is 2014 and Marsha and I will have been married 54 years in March. We like to tell everyone that four of them were happy. Unfortunately, Marsha's happy four don't correspond to my happy four.

Wow! Fifty-three years — who'd have thunk it? To our generation marriage is an institution and in order to get out of it, you have to prove you're sane, which neither of us can because living together this long proves we're crazy. I know we've lasted a half-century because we mutually realize that ours is truly a give-and-take relationship: She gives and I take! You think I say that to be funny but ask any of our friends. Marsha treats me as if I'm one of her children who must be coddled and protected. I married a fabulous, caring woman who mothers me, and I'm surely not going to tell her there might be a different style for our relationship — and don't you tell her either.

Over our years I've been a pretty good husband and father, give or take (see "give," "take" above) the 35,279 times I've landed on her &#%* list. Of those 35,279 times I have forgotten all but three. She, however, has categorized all those episodes into a list of worst to least in descending order and committed every one to her perfect memory. I wouldn't mind if she kept all those 35,279 disasters in the same order but she keeps rearranging them so I can never completely atone.

On our twenty-fifth anniversary our children, Kurt, Eric, Dina and Kira, threw us a surprise party with all our friends and a few enemies attending. It was a fabulous evening with movies, slide shows and lots of roasting of our years together. Marsha and I were impressed as there was tons of expensive food and drink for everyone and our kids had done a great job organizing it. A few days later I realized that I was paying most of my children's bills and I'd just thrown ourselves a great, expensive, surprise anniversary present.

On our fiftieth anniversary our children were all settling down. Three of the families had a couple of kids and since 2008 they were trying to keep their financial surfboards above the ebbing economic tide. Throwing a party for us was way beyond our kids' dusty bank accounts, but Eric, Dina and Kira organized a surprise anniversary gathering at the Steak Pit. Most of our group of friends attended and pitched in, and Marsha and I were treated to a fabulous evening with people we love. Eldest son Kurt was tied up with business obligations in California and had to miss the festivities but said he'd catch up later.

A few weeks later Kurt was able to come to Aspen and, true to Brendlinger form, he, our other children and grandkids, Remi, Camden, Chloe, Macie, Jack Jr. and Addie, decided to play a golden anniversary practical joke on their parents/grandparents. Kurt had prepared a challenging scavenger hunt and we had to decipher the clues. Our cobwebby minds were struggling and we needed additional verbal clues from the grandkids, like "Nana and Bampa, you guys are idiots — it's The Red Onion!" Kurt's clues led us to all the infamous places of our honeymoon disaster and other locations that were very important to our existence in Aspen: The Aspen Court, Red Onion, Ski Company, where both Marsha and I had worked, to the site of the torn-down Spider House that had been replaced by a 12-million-dollar duplex and to the site of our West Buttermilk family home for thirty-five years that was replaced by a 42-million-dollar mansion. Well, at least, we picked good lots.

Our last clue led us to The Applejack (now called the Aspen Mountain Lodge), the inn we had built in 1964 and ran for eleven years. It has been redeveloped into a condominium hotel with 39 units. Most of the units are much the same as what we built but now have one king bed, instead of two doubles, and a wet bar with refrigerator.

Our family had booked a night for Marsha and me in one of the elegant rooms as an anniversary gift. Funny, in all the years we owned and ran the inn, we had never spent a night in one of the units. Plus, Marsha hadn't been in the building since they had remodeled it in the mid-1990s. We were laughingly pleased that we were to spend a nostalgic night there.

It was strange that as we entered the lobby all our children and grandkids bid us a hasty adieu and quickly disappeared. We soon found out why. We opened the door to our unit to find it — surprise! — trashed. Stringers of colored crepe paper were everywhere, stretched between lamps, pictures, floors, TV, chairs, wet bar, ceilings, even the bath fixtures. There was more crepe paper in there than in Marsha's and my senior proms combined. The kids had to have started in the bathroom and then worked themselves toward the door of the room because there was absolutely no way to walk, slither or crawl through the maze of streamers. We laughed hysterically — they had gotten us, and good! But we didn't know the half of it. When we pulled down all the crepe paper we had two globs of it bigger than two exercise balls. Then we discovered that the bed had been short-sheeted and had a solid layer of apples under the mattress pad. There was an open bottle of '55 Dom Perignon and two champagne flutes on the nightstand, all empty! The light bulbs in the lamps and bath had been unscrewed. The shades on the lamps had been reinstalled upside down. The alarm clock was set for 4 a.m.

We realized that our offspring were chips-off-the-old-joker blocks as we giggled and laughed at everything that they had booby-trapped.

As delighted as I was to be the pigeon for a change, I enjoyed even more what I was told my 6-year-old grandson Jack Jr. said when he looked at the room fully draped in crepe paper, "I'm really worried about Bampa. How is he going to find his way to the bathroom in the middle of the night?"

CHAPTER 47

Bio of John McBride ... The Princeton Terror

Ever since hickory skis got a screw-on metal edge and seers decided to develop the perfect mountain snows of the Roaring Fork Valley, Aspen has been an irresistible magnet for the social elite, especially those hailing from east of the Mississippi. Sure, there was the occasional movie star from the la-la land of fruits and nuts and also scads of towheaded aliens from the upper Midwest — Minnesota, Wisconsin and even Chicago. These northern square-heads had frosty winters and liked skiing but had no sunshine, and Colorado's crystal-clear ultramarine blue skies were calling. But the real elite trekking toward Aspen were the prep-schooled, ivy-leagued aristocrats from the East Coast. Smart, attractive, confident and damn good skiers were pouring over the Castle Creek Bridge to find their sitzmarks in the growing drifts of opportunity.

Now don't get me wrong, we natives liked these aristocratic folks, BA's from Cornell, MBA's from Harvard, PhD's from Dartmouth, Yale or Princeton. They were bringing great ideas, lots of enthusiasm and, most important, a shit pot full of money. Compared to us ring-around-the-denim-collar Westerners, they appeared stuffy and sometimes acted so. But most of them threw the rep tie out the window or shook off the choker of pearls and let their hair down somewhere around North Platte, Nebraska. Now they were just trying to melt into the unsophisticated, classless Aspen mold.

And fit in they did. Aspen icons like Durrance, Pabst, Nitze, Metcalf, Beattie, Sterling, Whitcomb, Edel, Cole and many more left their ivy-covered schools or East Coast up-bringing and pulled on Aspen like a well-worn pair of longjohns.

John McBride was one of these Eastern elites that chose the West as his teething ring of adult existence. John was born and raised on the North Shore of Chicago but attended the elite prep schools in the East. He went to Princeton where he excelled in hockey, academics, hockey, pranks and hockey. John was an esteemed member of the 1961 National U.S. Hockey team. After college John went to California and worked with Owings Corning. There he met a Stanford beauty, Laurie Mack. He proposed and married her.

Laurie soon learned that you can't leave a door open to a prankster. John asked her what she wanted as a wedding present and since they'd just seen "Lawrence of Arabia," she flippantly said, "Oh, I don't know. How about a camel?" (I doubt she was thinking of camels when John quipped, "One hump or two?") John, of course, obliged and during their lavish reception he led a live, festooned camel into the hall and presented it to her as her wedding gift.

Laurie and John moved to Vail, a new resort, and, in those emerging environs John was a jack-of-all-trades. He assisted builder and developer George Shaw. He was also a cameraman for Summit Films and one of 18 ski instructors for Morrie Sheppard's original Vail Ski School.

John was invited to meet and ski with California developer, Bill Janss, whose corporation was going to build the huge base facilities at the new Aspen/Snowmass resort. That meeting went well and in 1966 John was hired as the Director of Commercial Development for the new village at the base of Snowmass.

I met John when the Howard Englander's and Brendlinger's decided to build a fondue restaurant in the new village and we were the first retail establishment to inquire about leasing. John was in charge of signing leases for the village and he presented us with a 20-page lease crammed full of very restrictive where-ases and what-ifs. Howard and

I read it over and agreed that it was way too restrictive for our small restaurant and decided to start the negotiations from a position of strength: We weren't going to agree to any of it. Except for a few whatevers, we redlined 90 percent of it expecting to eliminate only a few of the more insignificant restrictions. Howard, however, had recently been hired as Director of Marketing for Snowmass Village and most of the Janss executives had stayed in my lodge and had become close friends with Marsha and me, so we thought we might get some favorable considerations.

Howard and I were ready with an eloquent and convincing presentation for our "teeny little lease" negotiation. We nervously sat in John's office loaded with supportive charts and graphs. He walked in carrying our bled-on, marked-up lease. He glared at us; we gulped. He held it high and screamed, "You call this a lease? You've gotta be kidding me! There's hardly a word in here you haven't scratched out!" We gulped and gulped again! John slammed the document in the middle of his desk and yelled, "Sign it!" With wide eyes and shaky hands, we did, and the door burst open and all the Janss execs were there with champagne and big congratulatory smiles. We'd signed the first retail lease for the Snowmass Village.

This was our first clue that John was to be a master of the practical joke. The following stories are proof.

Open Wide:

John was good friends with Fabi and Fritz Benedict, Aspen iconoclasts. Fritz was instrumental in the alpine design and architecture of major ski areas in Colorado. John tells me Fabi was a wonderful jokester and he loved to turn the tables on her.

John was sitting in Bill Wesson's dental office having a filling repaired, and Fabi had the next appointment. She was ushered into Bill's dental chair in his second office. Fabi had no idea John was there and she settled comfortably into the chair waiting her turn. John didn't want to miss a prank opportunity so he convinced Bill to let him don a dental smock and mask, get a large pair of rusty Channel-Lock pliers from his truck, and appear in the other office masquerading as Dr. Bill Wesson, DDS.

He grunted a low "Hi, Fabi," and proceeded to roughly spin, tilt, raise and lower the chair several times while uttering, "Damn contraption!" A confused but unsuspecting Fabi opened her mouth wide when requested and then screamed "What the ... ?" when she saw the dirty, foot-long, plumbers' pliers John was trying to insert. Both Bill, standing outside the door, and John couldn't control it and burst out laughing and holding their sides. Once she realized it was John, even Fabi was laughing.

Cash Only:

John and architect Robin Molney noticed a real estate ad in the Wall Street Journal advertising a ranch near the new Snowmass. Faraway Ranch had been purchased by the Benedicts from Loey Rinquist, an ancient and delightful Aspen character. Loey lived like a recluse in a charming two-room homesteader's log cabin surrounded by her pride and joy, the most beautiful and colorful flower garden in the valley, if not the Western Slope. Loey was upset at all the growth going on and wanted to sell out and move to quieter, not yet developed, Telluride in the San Juan Mountains.

The Benedicts, for whatever reason, were not advertising the ranch locally but only in the Wall Street Journal. Realizing the prank possibility, John and Robin sent the Benedicts a telegram from a fictitious law firm in Connecticut stating they had a wealthy client who would buy the property, site unseen, for the full asking price. The only stipulation was that the closing would be on the ranch site in one week and the transaction was to be cash only. Two Connecticut lawyers would come to Snowmass to finalize the deal and the Benedicts were to meet them onsite at 1pm sharp. The Benedicts were a bit wary with such unusual conditions but they were also financially delighted at the quick turnover.

On the appointed day the anxious Benedicts were at the ranch site at 12:30. By 1:15pm there was not a sign of the lawyers. They waited 10 minutes, a half-hour, 45 minutes, a hour — nothing. They were quite worried and concerned, but it was 1967 and they were out in the sticks and there was no way to communicate with anyone. Finally along unpaved Brush Creek road came a big black Cadillac, billowing dust. The two lawyers were obviously being chauffeured as the Benedicts could see two well-dressed men in the back seat. The car stopped down the road, not wanting to negotiate the bumpy dirt driveway or get too close for the Benedicts to recognize anyone. The two distinguished gentlemen climbed from the Caddy wearing black sunglasses, black suits, black fedoras and carrying bulky briefcases. Bulky enough to be filled with stacks of cash!

They waved and the Benedicts eagerly waved back. Up the long driveway the lawyers approached the relieved, smiling couple. As they neared, the lawyers started to giggle and slap their knees. The dumb-struck Benedicts recognized the lawyers as their nasty "friends" John McBride and his sidekick Robin Molney, and in the bulging briefcases were a couple of six-packs of Coors.

Always Trust Your Electrician:

John also told me about a good prank and I probably won't re-member all the fine details but the story goes something like this.

After both their parents had passed away, John and his two sisters were riding the commuter train from North Chicago to the Loop to go to the bank to discuss some terms of the estate. Riding with them was their banker, a good friend and fellow Princeton graduate, Garland Lasater. He mentioned to John that he had a meeting with John's old Princeton roommate, Perry Lewis. John asked if Perry knew that he'd be in the bank at the same time, and Garland said no. John decided it was a great setup for a prank. Garland agreed.

When they got to the bank they opened a maintenance room and found some coveralls that had Earl the Electrician embroidered on the left chest pocket. There was also an old Chicago Cubs hat, a couple of florescent tube lights and an 8-foot stepladder to complete the prank kit.

John decked himself out as Earl the Electrician and waited in Garland's office for Perry to show up for his appointment. Perry arrived and after a few minutes reminiscing about their days at Princeton, Garland decided to get down to business

Garland: "OK, Perry, let's get right to it, I have another meeting at 11:15. So what are the terms of the proposed sale of your firm?"

Perry: "Well the offer is just under 5 million and our counter offer is 5.9 million."

Electrician (in a low grumbling tone but loud enough for Perry to hear): "WOW! That's a lot of moola for a dumb insurance company."

Perry: "What did he just say?"

Garland: "Oh, pay Earl no mind. He's been the electrician at this bank for 30 years and he is totally trustworthy."

Perry: "They are also making me an interesting offer of 4 million cash and a 25 percent interest in the firm."

Electrician: "Jeez, what an idiot this guy is, considering this volatile market, take the money and run!"

Perry jumps up and screams at the electrician: "Hey, you! You just shut the hell up. This is a private discussion and you have no right to butt in. Who in the hell do you think you are?"

The electrician turned slowly on the ladder, takes off the Chicago Cubs hat and says calmly, "Why, I'm your old roommate from Princeton, John McBride, and I don't know anything about being an electrician or high finances."

All around there was lots of hugging and laughter.

CHAPTER 48

More John McBride:

Rainless Rainbow:

Larry Yaw is a fabulous, talented Aspen architect and one of the nicest guys you'll ever meet. But nice guys make great patsies and Larry was a perfect victim for McBride's jokes.

It was the mid 1970's and the gay/lesbian movement across the nation was in full swing (good choice of words) and it seemed lots and lots of people were " peeking out" if not "coming out." Cosmopolitan Aspen had a small but eager presence of this rainbow community and they ran a weekly display ad in The Aspen Times stating,

GAY? New in town or just visiting? Call the Aspen Gay Hotline 925-6931

McBride noticed that the phone number rang a bell; it was just a couple of digits from the home phone of Larry Yaw, a coincidence John couldn't pass up. He called the Times ad department and convinced the lady that the phone number had been misprinted and it should read 925-6937 — a seven, not a one. She changed it and for a few weeks the erroneous ad ran with Larry's home phone number. Larry's phone was inundated with calls from swishy, indignant genders: "I don't understand, hon, why would you dare print that ad in the paper if you're not GAY? C'mon sweetie, aren't you surreptitiously trying to come out? Meet me at the J Bar for a brewski and we'll discuss it like good little girls!"

A Few Changes:

The Aspen Skiing Company allowed several local photography businesses to shoot photos of the skiers on the mountains so the skiers could order prints as keepsakes. One of those businesses was Walnut House, a photo shop on Galena Street. The proprietor of the shop was Rick Newton, a close friend of McBride's and John visited the shop often.

One day John was casually looking at all the photos on the wall and noticed a familiar face. He did a double take. There was his friend Larry Yaw skiing with a family who definitely was not Larry's family. But, wait ... he went for a magnifying glass. Wow, it wasn't Larry but a man whose likeness would fool Larry's mother, grandmother and the beautician who waxed his upper lip. Oh, this is too good. This picture was perfect for a prank.

Larry's a family man with a beautiful wife, Phyllis, and four great kids, Fletcher, Kendall, Kirsten and Lindsey and none of them re- motely resembled the wife or children in the photo. Perfect!

John and Rick concocted a classic prank. Rick enlarged the picture and they reproduced the image on a hundred Christmas cards and mailed them to Larry's family, friends and business acquaintances. The message inside read,

Merry Christmas and a Happy New Year to All My Dear Friends. Hope this card finds you and yours happy and well. Everything is fine here, but you might notice a few changes. Love, Larry

O M G —Those Are My Underwear:

Back in the 1960s and '70s there were two motorized lift routes to get to the top of Aspen's premiere ski mountain, Aspen Mountain, or as the locals like to call it, Ajax. One was up the Ruthie's side on Lift-1, a single chair, opened in 1946. It was a unique lift as not only was it the longest chairlift in the world but also it had a gate-like footrest with an attached flannel-lined canvas cover that you could pull over your legs and head to ward off the chill on the long 45-minute ride to the Sundeck. This antiquated chairlift, Aspen's first, was replaced by the double chair Lift-1A in 1972. The other way to the top was on the east side and was a combination of three double chairlifts. The first lift was up the short Little Nell hill, then you'd ski 100 yards to Lift No. 5, called the Bell Mountain Chair, and transfer again by skiing down to a third lift, called, well, Number 3.

Strange how some lifts are called by names, Ruthie's or Bell Mountain, and others just stay the number in which they were built. Anyway, in the pre-gondola years, it was a complicated multi-lift journey to get to the top. But it allowed the Ski Company to get the mad rush of morning skiers off the bottom and yet allow each of these access lifts to serve a skiing section of the mountain for the rest of the day.

Who would think that a chairlift would be the source of a prank? But some scallywag, womanizer riding the Bell Mountain Lift (No. 5) was anxious to show the world explicit evidence of his conquering ways, and he tossed a pair of bra and panties into an aspen tree below the first tower of the lift. Other Romeos thought that was hilarious and over the next few days that aspen tree became a decorated monument full of lacy underwear dangling from every limb. To no one's surprise it was appropriately named "The Panty Tree."

Naturally the rather staid Ski Company had their employees, using long expandable poles, remove the embarrassing garments. This Victorian, prudish response incensed a few of the town's jokesters, and over a keg's-worth of 10-cent beers at the Red Onion, they conspired to bring back the collection. John McBride and a few of his tongue-in-cheek pals, Bob Chamberlain, Tom Marshall and Fred Davies, planned a resurrection of that memorial tree. A couple of them went down to a Glenwood department store and purchased 150 pairs of cheap underwear. Most of it was women's dainties but to make the tree more universal, they bought a few men's jockeys and an enormous pair of women's bloomers a couple of axe handles wide. Ugh! These pillars of the community were panicked someone would recognize them with a cart full of unmentionables so they hid them under masculine tarps and coveralls and waited until a checkout line was completely clear.

At night the bloomer brigade climbed the mountain and decorated the tree with twenty or so undies and the next day the ski company removed them. After several nights of decoration and days of removal, the Ski Company surrendered and the Panty Tree became a permanent monument to Aspen's nocturnal revelry.

CHAPTER 49

And still more John McBride:

Honey, We're Invited:

Loved by everyone, twinkly-eyed, round-faced, grinning, cute, fun-loving Molly McKinnon went to work for McBride when he was developing the Airport Business Center. When tickled, Mollie had a giggle that was usually interrupted by an involuntary snort. That snort always erupted a laughing fit with all those in earshot.

Both Mollie and John were natural jokesters. Alone, each was a lovable nuisance but together they were absolute monsters of the prank. Their hilarious M.O. was the phony invitation. They'd pick an unsuspecting couple or business, have an invitation printed up that read something like this:

You are cordially invited to a Surprise 10th Anniversary Party for Marsha and Jack at their home on Snowbunny Lane on January 19th at 6pm sharp. It's potluck so bring hors d' oeuvres and a bottle of wine. Remember this is a surprise party so it's a secret! Don't RSVP, just show up!

They would mail this invitation to many people, making it a classic double prank, first on the unsuspecting couple whose anniversary was nowhere near that date, and, secondly, on all the surprised attendees.

But, you know, 9 times out of 10 it turned into a great party when no one could remember why they had gotten together in the first place.

Planet Hollywood:

This faux invitation prank worked as well on an unsuspecting business.

The 1991 grand opening in downtown Aspen for Planet Hollywood's elite Hard Rock Café backed by several movie stars, was going to be a fabulous affair with lots of celebrities in attendance and Oscar-like swinging searchlights, bleachers and a red carpet on South Galena Street.

Not to be upstaged, jokesters McBride and Rick Newton send out a fictitious invitation to a pre-grand opening party for the night before the actual opening. The invitation went something like this:

> Dear Mr. and Mrs. Brendlinger,
> Please be our special guest at a Pre-Grand Opening of the Fabulous Planet Hollywood at 7pm on Tuesday the 26th at our new location on Galena Street.
> This exclusive invitation will honor only the top thirty-five influential couples in Aspen. Please join us in celebrating our debut in Aspen by dressing as your favorite movie star.

Rick Newton's Walnut House camera and photo shop was directly across the street from Planet Hollywood's new location, and Rick, John and Molly wiped laughing tears from their eyes as car after car pulled up in front of the closed, dark restaurant. Opulently costumed and confused invitees banged on the locked door. "Let us in!" Bang! Bang! "Don't you know who we are?" **Bang! Bang! "We are the Aspen 35!"**

CHAPTER 50

Nobody Beats A Dealin' Tam's Used Car Deal ... Nobody!

Mr. and Mrs. E.R.Skelley

And

Mr. and Mrs. Fitzhugh Scott

Request the presence of your company

at the marriage of their children

Susan Skelley

And

Fitzhugh Scott III

So goes the standard formal wedding invitation, stiffly correct, elegantly embossed, printed or engraved in gold on linen card stock. Looking more like a tatted doily than an invitation, it has a foolish little gold ribbon tying nothing together but two small holes punched in the corner. And what is it with that little piece of transparent toilet paper? Oh, I get it, the father-of-the-bride is going to need them when he gets the bill.

In March 1969 Tam (née Fitzhugh) and Sue Scott were married in Aspen. They were a handsome couple. Tam was an eminent law-yer who looked, and acted more like a rail-thin, unsophisticated Tom Sawyer than a jury-intimidating Clarence Darrow. Tam wanted to look the part of a sophisticated country lawyer and he strutted about town in brown and tan saddle shoes, button-down shirts, pleated khakis and leather-elbowed tweeds — none of them ironed.

When he was a law student in Denver he lived with George Shaw, an aspiring contractor who often introduced Tam as his butler. Shaw and friend John McBride hung on Tam the stuffy butler-like nickname, "Meadows."

They say opposites attract and if Tam was a bit of a lawyerish Tom Sawyer, Sue was just the opposite and she was his Becky Thatcher, a perfect mate to counteract his attorney facade. Her mini-skirted beau-ty was not the demure bat-an-eye, paint-my-fence kind, but rather a slug-on-the-arm, hey-big-fella, catch-me-if-you-can charm. They were a fun happy couple and a great addition to the town's grow-ing young families. However, a leprechaun's crooked smile under a half-squinty eye suggested this was a couple full of mischief, whom couldn't be trusted as pillars of the community. But, as jokers usually are, they were often the brunt of the pranks of their "friends."

After their wedding, the Scotts flew off to the Caribbean for a few weeks of blissful honeymoon, unaware the friends they left behind were preparing a grandiose prank.

The Scotts owned a small house on Hopkins Street, just to the South of Aspen's popular Paepke Park with its miners-built rough log gazebo bandstand. A block off and in full view of Main Street, the Scott's location was perfect for what the pranksters were plan-ning. They were going to turn the Scott's front lawn into a garish, handy-dandy used-car lot.

The group of conspirators was John McBride, Chuck Cole, Roger Moyer and Jeff Platt. They contacted Eve Homeyer, Aspen's venerable mayor, and had her include the Aspen Police as part of the scam. Also in on it was the Scotts' house-sitter, a lanky, beautiful tennis player, Scotty Cooper (once a.k.a. Jacobs and now a.k.a. Leddy).

During the weeks of the honeymoon, the nasty jokers pushed, pulled or dragged every abandoned jalopy in the valley, some fifteen of them, and lined them up meticulously on the Scott lawn. The rusting, dilapidated cars were brightly decorated with crepe-paper stringers, multicolored flags and a boatload of blinking Christmas lights. There were prices painted in whitewash on the windshields — if one existed. The conspirators erected a string of bright flashing lights illuminating a huge, professionally painted banner between two trees, which announced **"Honest Tam's Used Cars ... CHEAP!"** Or, with Tam's well-known miserly reputation, it could have read, **"CHEAP Tam's Used Cars ... HONEST!**

There were even people milling around kicking tires and making offers.

It was a glorious prank and the jokesters were proud of their ingenuity and effort. Not only were the newlyweds shocked, but also no one would own up to it, so cheap Tam had to pay a wrecker to haul the junkers away.

CHAPTER 51

But You Can't Arrest Me – I'm The City Attorney!

Wedding pranks are always on the top of a pranksters list. Therefore I'd better include one concerning the Aspen City Attorney, Albert Kern, the City Manager, Leon Wurl, and several of the players you've met before.

The brunt of this story is Albert Kern, City Attorney. Albie was, and I guess still is, the epitome of a man's man. He was devilishly handsome with his russet-colored outdoorsman tan. Beneath his shockingly black curly hair, there was a sparkle of mischief in his good eye. A childhood accident had left him with a right glass eye that only added

217

to his already mysterious charm. Albie was superb gambler whose John Garfield-like brooding good looks, seen through a stream of smoke from his pipe, gave him an advantage over any opponent. Let's face it Albie had that manly aura that attracted women, an aura that most men would kill for.

In 1955 Albie graduated from law school at the University of Colorado. Not willing, just yet, to accept the dusty doldrums behind a desk or in the courtroom, he decided to follow a few more fun passions. So he moved to Aspen and was a ski patrolman and bartender for three years. In the summertime he was a deckhand on a three-master, or lugging shrimp on a Gulf Coast fishing boat, or cutting trees for a logging firm, or tooling it up for a Chicago construction firm before he decided to settle down a bit. In '59 he took a job as an attorney with a prominent Roaring Fork lawyer, Clint Stewart. He was Assistant District Attorney under John Wendt for four years. In 1969 the new Aspen City Manager, Leon Wurl, talked Albie into accepting the City Attorney position.

Single Albie was a man about town but his roving days were cut down to size by Sue Gauss, a gorgeous lass from Marblehead, Massachusetts, who'd moved to Aspen to ski when she was 19 years old. While fourteen years younger than Albie, this beautiful dark-haired woman was a perfect match for Albie's sureness. The woman could ski, and ski she did as a premiere PSIA-certified ski instructor for the Aspen Ski Company on challenging Aspen Mountain. There was little doubt by her peers and students that she was at the tiptop of her profession.

Sue and Albie dated for six years, and they announced their engagement at the Jerome Bar in early 1969. They were married in a formal ceremony at the Aspen Community Church on June 7. A reception for nearly everyone in Aspen was held at the Pomegranate Inn on the outskirts of town.

The festivities were well underway when two police cars with lights flashing and sirens blaring arrived, and policemen handcuffed Albie and dragged him screaming from the reception. No one knew what was happening, including the bride.

Knowing that this was probably some silly prank by his good friend and boss, Leon Wurl, Albie, nonetheless, was hauled downtown to police headquarters where the officers fingerprinted him and took a mug shot with a number across his chest. He was marched over to the courthouse and stood in front of two lawyer friends: Tam Scott, acting as his defense attorney, and Lenny Oates, as the presiding judge. Lenny said, 'How do you plead?" Tam, his defense, said that Albie was totally guilty in whatever the charge was and Judge Oates, sentenced Albee to fifty years of blissful marriage for heinous crime of Contributing to the Delinquency of a Minor.

The whole process took about one-and-a-half hours and since irate Sue was not in on the joke, Albie already had a lot of "esplainin' " to do.

CHAPTER 52

Nobody Ever Said A Prankster
Had To Be Human

Tam Scott was infamous in Aspen. Yes, he was a good father, recognized lawyer, astute judge, and he had enough individual character to rank him high with the best of characters in a character-inundated town. But he couldn't hold a candle to the character that masqueraded as his dog: the incomparable Alabaster Smith.

Tam was given the dog by an old girlfriend, Pat Smith.

Alabaster Smith was a strikingly stark-white malamute.

Like a gigantic snowball, he stood some proud five hands high and if you looked carefully at his snow colored face you'd swear he was smiling. He was smiling because he knew, and I think Tam knew, Alabaster was the master of both the four-legged and two-legged world.

Aspen was practically overrun with dogs. You weren't anybody unless you had both a scruffy broom and scruffy dog in the back of your pickup. The town fathers were always trying semiserious ways to keep the dogs in check. In the 1960's, 70's and 80's they were laughingly unsuccessful. Everyone had a pet dog, including the politicians who feinted control and the police who were expected to uphold the weak leash laws. Therefore, un-tethered, both figuratively and accurately,

Alabaster could, and did, reign over everyone and everything.

His hoodwinked friend and feeder, Tam Scott, had his law office on the second floor of the Wheeler Opera House, smack in the middle of downtown. Typical of old brick buildings built in the Victorian era of the late 1800's, the Wheeler had tall crowned windows with extra wide stone sills that were a perfect perch for Alabaster. With a signature bright red bandana tied around his neck, he'd lie there every day and survey all that he controlled, his kingdom. Alabaster would occasionally flick an ear at someone he recognized or bark furiously at any dog encroaching on his territory. When the fire siren blew at noon, Alabaster took this as his musical cue to join in with a boisterous howl that he thought was in perfect harmony.

One nice sunny winter afternoon a lonely-looking female dog wandered into Alabaster's realm, and he thought he'd take the opportunity to pull a practical joke. He scurried from his perch and through the opera house memorizing sweet nothings he'd whisper in this comely bitch's ear. After a couple of get-to-know-you circles and sniffs, Alabaster and his new sweetheart did the "nasty" right there in the middle of the busy mall. Alabaster knew someone would get a picture of it, and somebody did.

That photo became famous all over the world as the photographer made it into a poster with the words, **"Have Your Next Affair in Aspen"**

Back on his window perch, Alabaster Smith was smiling, he'd gotten the recognition his kingly status deserved.

CHAPTER 53

City Sewer Line Hoax

John Keleher is a saint. No, it's not just me who thinks that. Ask anyone who has been in Aspen for more than a decade. He's the most caring and nicest man as you'll ever meet. John was inducted into the Aspen Hall of Fame in January 2012 — an honor well deserved. Perhaps his saintly character stems from the fact that he was a chin whisker away from the priesthood. With his continued good deeds, he is as close to a layman Catholic priest as a man can be. But somewhere in his saintly persona there lies a small gene, a gene that spawns a mischievous side of John that rivals that of an impish Irish leprechaun. Most of his practical jokes are classics.

John's a native New Mexican, married to Linda, and with their three boys, John Jr., Chris and Brian, they moved to Aspen in 1972 from Albuquerque. A former Navy Seabee (Construction Battalion) officer, John also gained a lot of construction knowhow building in Albuquerque. Thus, he was hired to assist the Janss Corporation's Chief-Engineer, Chuck Vidal, and oversee all the construction details of the ongoing Snowmass Base Village.

A few years later John stepped out on his own and became an owner's representative by overseeing an owner's interest in the confusing construction process. There are very few big Aspen buildings built in the last 30 years that John hasn't been the owner's representative: Harris Hall, the new Benedict Music Tent, The Little Nell hotel, the Aspen firehouses, the Library, the gondola terminals, and numerous private homes.

One of John's projects, The Little Nell hotel, led to one of his pranks. For many years there was a bar and restaurant at the bottom of Little Nell ski slope on Aspen Mountain. Naturally, the base bar was called "Little Nell" and it was internationally famous for its huge open-air deck on the mountain side that was a gathering spot like no other on Earth. Thousands of beautiful people from Aspen and from all over assembled there after skiing for pitcher after pitcher of Coors Draft, while searching for a comely date for the evening. It was said that if you couldn't get a date at the Nell deck, then you probably looked like Toulouse-Lautrec in drag.

The old Little Nell was a nondescript wood building painted an exciting oxford brown. There were a few parking places but it seemed as if it were just crammed in at the bottom of the ski run, and most everyone thought nothing of any substance could be built there in its place. Wrong!

The venerable Aspen Ski Company was looking to expand their business from an uphill transportation company to one with hotels, restaurants, shops and valet parking. They bought and tore down the old Little Nell bar and restaurant and, unbelievably, on that postage-stamp-sized property was built one of the finest five-star hotel/restaurant/shopping complexes in any city, let alone a little ole mountain ski town.

As you can imagine, building a first-class hotel with 92 rooms, three restaurants, banquet facilities for 500, an outdoor swimming pool and underground valet parking garage was going to be a huge undertaking, and the construction activity was going to disrupt the neighborhood for a long, long time.

In the neighborhood was Tom Anderson and his Pomeroy Sports retail ski and sports shop right across the street. Now he and the Little Nell project's owner's rep, John Keleher, were longtime bosom buddies. In fact, John physically helped Tom build his house up in Meadowood. Tom couldn't resist venting his frustration at the cacophony of cranes, bulldozers, jackhammers and dump trucks that bombarded he and his customers' senses and disrupted his small shop. Of course Tom knew that a new luxury hotel right across the street would eventually be good for his business. However, it was still an aggravating situation, so every couple of days he'd march over to the construction office and browbeat John about when was the damn project going to be over!

Finally, the construction was coming to an end and Tom was elated to get the area back to normal. But John couldn't pass up a chance for a great prank and while he was in the town's Utility Department John picked up a piece of the department's blank stationery and an accompanying envelope.

Using a typewriter, John addressed an official-looking letter to all those businesses along East Durant Street. The letter informed the businesses (only mailed to Tom's shop, of course) that the city needed to replace the sewer line along East Durant and that it would be a major project that might last as long as a year or even eighteen months. The City was asking for the indulgence of the businesses for any inconvenience they may have to endure. The letter was signed by a facsimile and misspelled signature of the current Utility Department

Tom was livid! After years of construction, how could the City do this? He grabbed the letter and marched down to City Hall to raise hell. He demanded to see the Mayor, City Manager, and Utility Department head. It took several minutes of Tom's ranting and raving before the manager began to understand what the hell he was talking about.

"Tom, calm down, let me see if I understand you. You think we are building a new sewer line down East Durant Street?"

Tom, waving the letter, screamed, "Of course you are. Here is the damn letter you sent me!" And he threw the letter down on the desk.

The manager assured Tom that the city was not doing any sewer work. He had not written the letter and it was a hoax. Tom had been had and sulked back to the store.

One of his employees looked at the letter and said, "This has Keleher written all over it!" Indeed it did!

CHAPTER 54
Crossing the Hudson

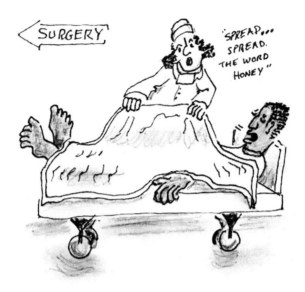

Aspen doesn't have a lot of black residents, and I'm guessing there have never been many. Sure there have been a few and they have been important contributors to our society. One such group was the Bernie Hudson family who moved here in 1969. Bernie, the patriarch, brought his family here from Chicago to open a barbershop and hair salon. Although most Aspenites didn't get their hair cut very often, Bernie's engaging personality, extraordinary sense of humor and hair expertise made him an immediate success. Even if you didn't need it, you went in to get a trim just so you could enjoy the bantering and jokes wafting back and forth between Bernie, the customer in the chair and the numerous hangers-on who were there for the camaraderie.

Bernie was on the smaller side, sort of an Aspen version of Sammy Davis Jr. He was also a gifted athlete and the high school coaches were excited for the Hudson kids to grow enough to play on their teams. Bernie played on our softball and broomball teams a few times and we loved his locker-room jock humor.

But the trait that made Bernie's humor even more hysterical was that he stuttered. Not the kind of stutter where the speaker just can't get a word out, like trying to say "darn." "D... d ... d ... d ... d ... ah er... Rats!" Bernie would get stuck on the whole word. A Rams' fan, he'd say: "Those Broncos...Broncos...Broncos are a sad bunch ... bunch ... buuunch ... ofdonkeypoop!" The last three words were blurted rapid fire as one word. If his stutter bothered him, he never let on — Bernie just used it to emphasize his punch lines.

One day Bernie nervously announced, "Janice and I got ... got ... got ... gotenoughkids. I'm going to have ... have ... have ... have ... mypeckerplugged!"

On the afternoon of his outpatient operation, we all showed up at his shop, anxious to hear the gory details. The doctor knew that Bernie was very nervous about the procedure and had planned a practical joke.

Bernie stripped and laid down on the operating table. As the elderly nurse shaved the target area, proud Bernie said, "Honey, it's OK by me if you just spread ... spread ... spread ... thewordaroundtown!"

From behind Bernie, the conniving doctor said, "Hope you're ready, Bern, as this is going to hurt a bit." And, with a nasty Frankenstein grin, he stepped around and beside Bernie, holding in one hand a huge foot-long hypodermic needle used on horses and a lumberjack's bow saw in the other.

Bernie's eyes leapt to Frisbee size and he shouted,

"BAALLS...BAALLS...BAALLS...BACK TO CHICAGO!

And then he fainted!

CHAPTER 55

You Can't Steal a Cop Car! Oh Yeah, Just Watch!

N othing was off-limits when nasty, always conniving Ken Sterling and "Toilet Seat" Hoff were together.

Both of them knew Gary Wall, a young, very likable deputy sheriff in the Pitkin County Sheriff's Department in Aspen. Gary was handsome, very bright and personable, and it didn't take long for the community to welcome him. His likeability, however, meant that he would probably be moving on to higher paying police jobs. Shortly after he'd won over our community, it was bye-bye Gary, and he was hired to be Vail's new police chief.

A few months later Toilet Seat and Ken decided to go skiing over in Vail and possibly stop and say hi to Gary. As they drove into Vail they saw Gary getting out of his squad car and go into the 7-Eleven, pre-sumably to get coffee and the token donut. In the time it took to pull a U-ey and drive up in front of the convenience store, they realized Gary had left his squad car running.

Ken smirked at Hoff, and Hoff screamed, "You can't steal a cop car!" "Oh yeah? Just watch me," Ken replied. He jumped out of the car, slid behind the wheel and stealthily eased the squad car out of the parking lot. Ken drove the car into an adjoining subdivision while turning on and off the siren, just for the fun of it. He pulled the car to the curb, left it running, and leapt back into Hoff's car and said like a true Aspenite, "Let's go ski this crummy area!"

Now, what Ken and Hoff didn't realize is that policemen are smart and accustomed to solving crimes. Plus, they have a pot full of infor-mation available. It didn't take Chief Wall's officers long to find his car, and Gary recognized this as a probable prank. Since Gary was new to Vail and knew few people, he deduced this might be a prank from two well-known pranksters from Aspen, nasty Ken Sterling and Toilet Seat Hoff. He had his dispatcher request the license plate numbers of both these gentlemen and then had his patrolmen drive through the Vail parking lots searching for either number. Aha, there was Hoff's car, as suspected.

Still quite pleased with themselves, the pranksters finished skiing and discovered that their car had disappeared from the lot. Stolen? Perhaps. But a better solution might be confiscated. Damn!

Sterling and Hoff dragged their skis and paraphernalia five long blocks to the police station, and, tails between their legs, crawled into the station to meet their fate. Touché.

CHAPTER 56

Whew! It's Gonna Get Hot in Here!

Beautiful Chuck and Sally Cole were wonderful additions to the Aspen community. While they are no longer a married item, they individually are still very important to the area.

Chuck met Sally, a debutante from (Oh, my, look at those pearls!) Shaker Heights, Ohio. They moved from Wayzata, Minnesota, in the mid-1960s with their terrific three daughters, Lisa, Sarah and Gretchen. I've already mentioned that our group liked to go to dinner and then go to the Tippler or The Knight Club for a few more bumps and dancing to the fabulous Walt Smith Trio. Sally liked to party and Chuck would rather be home sleeping, so along about 9:30 Chuck would yawn and announce that he needed to go home to bed but Sally was welcome to stay on with us. Then, in keeping with his ability to stretch a dollar, he would throw a dollar and some loose change on the table and say that ought to cover Sally's share. He smiled as he left because he knew he would save a ton on babysitter fees if he went home early.

There was no need for this behavior as he and Sally could afford whatever they wanted. After all, they had built a beautiful, expensive home on the slopes of Starwood, where they were neighbors of John Denver.

Our meager house on Buttermilk Mountain was directly across the Roaring Fork Valley from Starwood and using a surveyor's tool I was able to determine that our house was, indeed, 1.8 feet higher than theirs. I never let him forget that I was always looking down on him.

Years later they bought a fantastic ranch at the end of Hook's Lane in Basalt. It was a former fish hatchery and was dotted with intricate patterns of silvery ponds where big fish crisscrossed the shining surfaces. They must have spent a ton for it because they named it Rock Bottom Ranch.

It was a spectacular piece of real estate and they built an incredible ranch house to do the property justice.

To show off their brand-new digs, the Coles hosted several gatherings and would invite a few of their friends to a cozy dinner and tour. One night's entourage was Tom and Janny Anderson, the honorable Judge Tam and Sue Scott, and Mary Ann and Peter Greene.

Chuck had outfitted his living room with a powerful new woodburning stove called a Rumsford. Chuck couldn't wait for guests so he could brag about this great moneysaving, heat-producing device.

As his guests dutifully sat on his couch with hands in laps, Chuck gave them a lesson in expert fire building in his new Rumsford. His guests were enthralled, not with the stove, but with Chuck's rampant enthusiasm for a wood-burning stove.

Dissertation over and a fire burning enthusiastically in the Rumsford, Chuck retired to the kitchen to help Sally with the pu-pus and drinks. When they returned with trays they were stunned, there sat all their guests sitting on the couch, hands in laps, and in one state of shocking near nudity or another. They all yelled in unison, "Whew! It sure is gonna get hot in here!"

CHAPTER 57

Opportunity Knocks

Sometimes something will crop up that feeds an already germinating joke.

That was the case between good friends Charlie Cole and Tom Anderson. They were displaced Minnesotans who had come to Aspen because the snow, the mountains and weather were much nicer than in freezing, flat and dreary Minnesota. They were buddies in Minnesota and they remained so after moving west.

Tom was the very successful owner-operator of the popular Pomeroy Sports, across from the gondola. His wife, Janny, had a fine ladies lingerie shop called the Freudian Slip located in the same building. They built a new house in Meadowood, an area that started modestly but soon became a very prestigious subdivision.

Charlie and his wife, Sally, after many years living in town and then up in Starwood, a subdivision that started out prestigious and only got more that way, bought a fantastic ranch down in Emma that they endearingly named Rock Bottom Ranch.

After building a grandiose home on the ranch, Charlie was given the honey-do chore of clearing the ranch of old dilapidated farm equipment. He'd hired a flatbed truck with a winch and was making several trips to the dump.

He was finally down to his last load, an old rusty Jeep of World War II ilk and it had seen its best days around that time. All the tires were rotted and flat, and the windshield was long since broken out. The hood was gone and over the years songbirds had built numerous straw nests on the oil-blackened motor. If ever there was an eyesore, this old wreck was it.

Because it was so ugly and already up on the flatbed — BINGO — opportunity knocked, and Charlie couldn't resist. In the dead of night he delivered that monstrosity to the front yard of Tom's new house in Meadowood. He was pleased with himself because he knew Tom would have to pay someone to haul the mess to the dump.

However, all good pranks will also leave the prankster at risk for a "Get Even!"

Charlie had been developing real estate for several years, and one of his commercial buildings was in the industrial park across from the airport. The park was developed by John McBride, whom you've met before in this chronicle. Because John is so creative, he named his development across from the airport the Airport Business Center, and because he went to Princeton, John needed something he could remember and he shortened it to the ABC.

Charlie built a nice building to house offices for the growing businesses of Aspen. He also built an office on the second floor for himself that was conveniently on the south side of the building with a nice large deck overlooking a great view of the Aspen Rent-All equipment yard and the kennels of veterinarian Craton Burkholder.

Charlie's large deck was the Get Even opportunity for Tom, so he hired Myers & Company, a large welding and industrial iron company, whose owner was a good friend and, more important, he had a healthy-sized crane.

With the help of the crane and the dark of night, they lifted that ugly jeep carcass and gently placed it on Charlie's beautiful office deck for one and all to admire.

Now guess who had to pay to remove it?

CHAPTER 58

Nutty Barbara Moebius

Where can I start with a character as crazy and nutty as Barbara Moebius? Barbara passed on a couple of years ago, and at the overflowing celebration of her life, friend after friend stood up to tell the zany, hysterical things they remembered about her. You'd had thought you were at a comedy fest instead of a memorials service.

Marsha and I met Barbara and Dick and their fine family when they moved to Aspen to build the Silvertree Inn at the new Snowmass Ski Area, just eight miles from Aspen. As I've told you before, they moved into the other side of the Spider House duplex on Snowbunny Lane and we became quick and lifelong friends — but everyone Barbara ever met became a quick and lifelong friend. She was infectious! She was a lightning wit and just plain damn funny.

Not one for fancy things Barbara was as comfortable in a flowered cotton housedress as Jackie O was in a pillbox hat.

Other than getting her cat to drop live mice at Marsha's feet, she wasn't so much a practical joker as she was a joker with everyone. Each of her friends had their own little joke with Barbara. Mine was an endless series of mailed note cards, each of them very funny about some rubber duckies.

When I was Rotary president in 1991 I started a rubber ducky race in the Roaring Fork River as a fundraiser for the youth groups in the valley. The fundraiser is still going after 23 years, and it has raised over three million dollars. Every year the youth groups and Rotary members sell between 25,000 to 30,000 ducks at an average of $8 each, and they dump them all into the river for a race of about mile through the center of town. It's a family festive affair and I only mention it because it is the basis of a joke between Barbara and me, and, yes, I am kind of proud of it and the Rotary Club that organizes the Rubber Ducky race year after year.

Barbara would call me up every August to buy $25 worth of ducks, six I believe it was. After the first year she was astonished that I hadn't called her and told how much she'd won. I explained that her chances to win were 6 in 30,000.

She wrote me a card stating she wasn't buying any more ducks until her odds went up. I wrote her a card that if she'd buy $50 worth she would double her chances. She did and still she didn't win anything. Another card stated that since I was the head duck in charge certainly there was something I could do. I wrote back that if she bought $75 worth of ducks, I would personally train them for 30 days prior to the race and those little ducks would be so fast nothing could stop them. Just before the race I sent a card telling her how many pushups, sit-ups and laps her ducks did in the Olympic pool and what good shape they were in.

After the race when I didn't call she sent me a card with one word: Well?? I returned a card and apologized that I had over trained and overfed her ducks and they petered out 100 yards from the finish line. The next summer Barbara sent a nasty card stating "I was to train them under strict Moebius rules: No more than three sit-ups, two pushups, two laps in the toilet and one roll in the hay, plus a diet consisting of ½ kernel of corn per day."

After the race I sent her a card saying that when the ducks hit the cold river water those half-kernels of corn blew up to a full potion of cornpone and they all drowned 18 ½ inches from the starting line.

The next year the training and diet were perfected and she knew she'd win. The day after the race and before I got the "Well??" card, I came upon the perfect response. Knowing Barbara's fond inclinations towards animals, especially cats, I drew a picture of a very fat cat and explained that when her ducks were well out in front, swimming in formation, and quacking in cadence, an obviously starving pussy cat jumped in the water and ate every damn one of her ducks.

After that Barb still bought ducks but just sent me a card with a list of lame excuses for me to check off and send back. She never won a sou — but it was for a good cause.

The Lohrs, Behrhorsts, Chapins, Lights, Thorpes and Moebiuses had a weekly tennis match, and after the contests they went to a designated player's house for a potluck dinner. One evening it was the Thorpes' turn for the potluck. The tables were cleared and dishwasher running smoothly. As everyone was at the front door, Barb snuck back in the kitchen and stole every piece of silverware, and I mean everything, not even a pickle fork was left, and hid all of it under the bed in the guestroom. The Thorpes knew Barbara well enough to know she was the culprit. She innocently shrugged, "Moi?" Before the Thorpes found their silver, they had to buy plastic forks, spoons and knives.

Afraid no one would remember, Barbara threw herself a birthday party every year. It was always a cross-country skiing picnic, held in the trees at the bottom of Sinclair Divide. She'd invite all her lady friends (and that was a gaggle) and demanded they all come in costume. It was a hilarious party with lots of laughs. One of those laughs was because Barbara would set out a different ski course each year, and on the day before the party she would hide wine jugs along the way. Unfortunately, she could never remember where she'd hidden them!

That was our Barbara, God rest her funny soul.

CHAPTER 59

Freddie "Schnicklefritz" Fisher
Aspen's Infamous Houdini

This is my wife's favorite practical joke, so I better include it in this chronicle.

As mentioned, we had built a lodge in Aspen, The Applejack Inn. Since we were on Main Street and also a member of the Best Western Chain, we were mostly full every summer night.

At least a couple of times a summer we were hosts to a busload of Iowa schoolteachers on a tour of the Rockies. Now when I say schoolteachers, these were a movie caster's dream as they couldn't have looked more like middle-aged schoolmarms, because that's just what they were. Seriously, they were 50 plus, all with grey hair, wearing sturdy lace-up black walking shoes over knee-high dark nylons. All wore nice lightly starched flowered dresses with crochet collars and cuffs and clutching, not wearing, but clutching white vinyl purses to their chests. And there were 44 of them on each bus.

My wife, Marsha, was an ex-schoolteacher and so she took it as a duty to squire these ladies around beautiful Aspen and show them the sights. One day she had a group of them in the new downtown mall, where often there were music students playing string quartets. On this particular day, Aspen's infamous and irreverent character Freddie "Schnickelfritz" Fisher was scrounged on the back of a card table chair playing a mean jazz coronet.

Not knowing Freddie's reputation as Aspen's resident curmudgeon, the schoolmarms were thrilled to hear such glorious music come from this troll-like character. They didn't know that here was a musician's musician who had one time had a band, Freddie Fisher and his Schnickelfritz Band, which had appeared in more than fifteen Hollywood movies. His band was the precursor to Spike Jones' looney band.

The story was that Freddie got in trouble with the IRS and when they began to garnishee his earnings, he moved his family to Aspen and did everything for cash only, including repairing anything, gold-plating Aspen leaves and, of course, playing the horn at Kuster's Red Onion Bar and Restaurant.

The schoolmarms were enthralled and were dropping money in the box at the bottom of his feet. After a couple of numbers he said, "That's all, folks," and began to climb off his perch. All forty-four ladies yelled "Encore, encore," trying to applaud without losing control of their white vinyl handbags clutched to their chests. Freddie said no encore but he'd be glad to do his favorite magic trick for them. And the schoolmarms in unison said, "Oh, please do, Mr. Fisher!"

Freddie grinned a toothless smile, tipped his ever-present porkpie hat, and pulled a semi-clean handkerchief from his jacket pocket. He made a fist with his right hand and put the hanky over that fist with a few abracadabras. He pulled the hanky off his fist and there was his fist with his index finger extended. He then carefully put the hanky over his erect index finger and with a few abra whatevers, he pulled the hanky off and his index finger was gone (no longer erect). Then, of course, he made a fist with his left hand and put the hanky over that fist, said a few more magic incantations —TA DA! — and yanked the hanky off to reveal a beautiful middle finger as he gave forty-four agape schoolmarms the bird. TA DA!

Tour guide Marsha knew irreverent Freddie well, and she had to bite hard on her cheek to stifle a guffaw.

CHAPTER 60
ASPEN STATE TEACHERS COLLEGE

Courtesy of Aspen State Teachers College

No chronicle of Aspen practical jokes would be complete without a chapter on the infamous and fictional Aspen State Teachers College.

In the mid-1970s three very funny entrepreneurial Aspenites, Dr. Slats Cabbage, aka Marc Demmon; Fulton Begley III, aka Al Pendorf; and Harold Center aka Jim Furniss, pulled off a joke, not only on Aspen but also on the whole country. They created the Aspen State Teachers College (ASTC), listed as the **No Classes, No Credit, Fun College of the Rockies.** It was a mastermind concept and it was an idea that had endless possibilities for merchandising and craziness.

I was already too old to imbibe in the hilarious campus activities but I could sit back and enjoy all the craziness and envy those guys who could pull off such an ingenious ruse.

Cabbage, Begley III and Center, the trio of campus deans,

presidents, chancellors or whatever, didn't let any merchandising concept go unturned. They had T-shirts, baseball caps and beer mugs emblazoned with the college coat-of-arms that was a logo consisting of a pair of skis, a mug of suds, a broom and a leaf that I think was an aspen leaf, but given that loose hippy era I'm not sure what kind of leaf it was supposed to be.

They published a successful weekly newspaper called the Clean Sweep that included hilarious campus news, lists of ridiculous classes, and non-existing events. One I remember the most was their published football schedule for the coming season and it looked something like this:

Sept. 25, ASTC vs. Notre Dame (Home Game)
Sept. 30, ASTC vs. Ohio State (Home Game)
Oct. 5, ASTC vs. UCLA (Home Game)
Oct. 12, ASTC vs. Stanford (Home Game)
Oct. 19, ASTC vs. Alabama (Home Game)
Oct. 26, Bye week
Nov. 2, ASTC vs. Michigan (Home Game) Homecoming:
Nov. 9, ASTC vs. Nebraska (Home Game)
Nov. 16, ASTC vs. Oklahoma (Home Game)

Every week they published the game results sort of like this:

Once again the ASTC Fighting Brooms continued their winning streak as the scaredy-cat Nebraska Cornhuskers failed to show up at Wagner Park and therefore forfeited to the unbeaten Brooms.

Via the forfeit the Brooms' record is now 7 and 0, the best in the country, and they are looking forward to hosting a major bowl game.

"Sweep em up and sweep em out — go Brooms"

To keep their students entertained ASTC had several activities to keep up the spirits (beer, wine and vodka). There was a bowling contest in the mall using an empty beer keg as a ball and freshmen as the pins.

There was a broom ball soccer game in Wagner Park using a beach ball and the ratty ole brooms that were the school's mascot.

Most hilarious was the three-legged race where the hapless contestants had to race from bar to bar drinking a beer each before they could go to the next bar. In those days, well ever since Aspen was founded there were lots of bars, so the contestants had their fill and lots of falls before a pair of sloshes were awarded the trophy.

For classical entertainment there was a marching band with kazoos and pots and pans as the major instruments, and the ASTC Band was in every community parade.

The ASTC was unique; national media picked up the story and the bogus college became a national phenomenon.

And I thought, "Damn, why didn't I think of that?

Epilogue

These stories, most of them happening some 30 or 40 years ago, have been told numerous times around the dinner table. Some are short and funny and others long and past the border of boredom. All of them come from someone's ancient memory so some of the facts are hazy. All of our fuzzy memories would collectively apologize if we could remember what we are apologizing for.

This compilation could have been much longer because every time someone heard I was writing a practical-joke book, they seemed to have a favorite story from their past. I've been at this on and off for more than a year, and I just needed to stop at some point. I apologize to those of you who didn't get included, just as I'm apologizing to many of my friends who did get in and wished they hadn't.

I do want to thank all of you who have helped to keep me on a loose and rambling track. I pity Sara Garton, editor extraordinaire, who had to tangle with all the dangling participles and incomplete sentences. But, pity or not, she did a fantastic job.

Thanks also to my glorious wife, Marsha, who would take valuable time away from nursing me and baking cookies for the universe to help with my grammar and sometimes trying to keep my story telling somewhat close to reality.

And thanks to long-time friend, Ann Kevin for catching the uncrossed t's and missing commas.

The publishing firm of this effort made the suggestion that this book be marketed as a perfect **bathroom reader**. They could print it on thin perforated tissue therefore assuring that it could be eventually put to good use.

I'm not dead yet and I still like to play a joke or two when you least expect it. So, in parting, let me steal a quote from Satchel Paige:

"Don't look behind you, because someone might be gaining on you!" — and it's probably me!

Be very aware...and if a joke is played on you remember...you can always **Get Even.**

CAIO

CPSIA information can be obtained at www.ICGtesting.com
Printed in the USA
LVOW12s0835220115

423886LV00002B/3/P